There are a number of HORIZON CARAVEL BOOKS published each year. Titles now available are:

BEETHOVEN
THE SEARCH FOR KING ARTHUR
CONSTANTINOPLE, CITY ON THE GOLDEN HORN
LORENZO DE' MEDICI AND THE RENAISSANCE
MASTER BUILDERS OF THE MIDDLE AGES
PIZARRO AND THE CONQUEST OF PERU
FERDINAND AND ISABELLA
CHARLEMAGNE
CHARLES DARWIN AND THE ORIGIN OF SPECIES
RUSSIA IN REVOLUTION
DESERT WAR IN NORTH AFRICA
THE BATTLE OF WATERLOO
THE HOLY LAND IN THE TIME OF JESUS
THE SPANISH ARMADA
BUILDING THE SUEZ CANAL
MOUNTAIN CONQUEST
PHARAOHS OF EGYPT
LEONARDO DA VINCI
THE FRENCH REVOLUTION
CORTES AND THE AZTEC CONQUEST
CAESAR
THE UNIVERSE OF GALILEO AND NEWTON
THE VIKINGS
MARCO POLO'S ADVENTURES IN CHINA
SHAKESPEARE'S ENGLAND
CAPTAIN COOK AND THE SOUTH PACIFIC
THE SEARCH FOR EARLY MAN
JOAN OF ARC
EXPLORATION OF AFRICA
NELSON AND THE AGE OF FIGHTING SAIL
ALEXANDER THE GREAT
RUSSIA UNDER THE CZARS
HEROES OF POLAR EXPLORATION
KNIGHTS OF THE CRUSADES

American Heritage also publishes
AMERICAN HERITAGE JUNIOR LIBRARY
books, a similar series on American history.
Titles now available are:

FRANKLIN DELANO ROOSEVELT
LABOR ON THE MARCH, THE STORY OF AMERICA'S UNIONS
THE BATTLE OF THE BULGE
THE BATTLE OF YORKTOWN
THE HISTORY OF THE ATOMIC BOMB
TO THE PACIFIC WITH LEWIS AND CLARK
THEODORE ROOSEVELT, THE STRENUOUS LIFE
GEORGE WASHINGTON AND THE MAKING OF A NATION
CAPTAINS OF INDUSTRY
CARRIER WAR IN THE PACIFIC
JAMESTOWN: FIRST ENGLISH COLONY
AMERICANS IN SPACE
ABRAHAM LINCOLN IN PEACE AND WAR
AIR WAR AGAINST HITLER'S GERMANY
IRONCLADS OF THE CIVIL WAR
THE ERIE CANAL
THE MANY WORLDS OF BENJAMIN FRANKLIN
COMMODORE PERRY IN JAPAN
THE BATTLE OF GETTYSBURG
ANDREW JACKSON, SOLDIER AND STATESMAN
ADVENTURES IN THE WILDERNESS
LEXINGTON, CONCORD AND BUNKER HILL
CLIPPER SHIPS AND CAPTAINS
D-DAY, THE INVASION OF EUROPE
WESTWARD ON THE OREGON TRAIL
THE FRENCH AND INDIAN WARS
GREAT DAYS OF THE CIRCUS
STEAMBOATS ON THE MISSISSIPPI
COWBOYS AND CATTLE COUNTRY
TEXAS AND THE WAR WITH MEXICO
THE PILGRIMS AND PLYMOUTH COLONY
THE CALIFORNIA GOLD RUSH
PIRATES OF THE SPANISH MAIN
TRAPPERS AND MOUNTAIN MEN
MEN OF SCIENCE AND INVENTION
NAVAL BATTLES AND HEROES
THOMAS JEFFERSON AND HIS WORLD
DISCOVERERS OF THE NEW WORLD
RAILROADS IN THE DAYS OF STEAM
INDIANS OF THE PLAINS
THE STORY OF YANKEE WHALING

A HORIZON CARAVEL BOOK

THE VIKINGS

By the Editors of
HORIZON MAGAZINE

Author
FRANK R. DONOVAN

Consultant
SIR THOMAS D. KENDRICK
Former Keeper of British Antiquities, British Museum

ILLUSTRATED WITH DRAWINGS, ILLUMINATIONS,
CARVINGS, AND MAPS, MANY OF THE PERIOD

Published by American Heritage Publishing Co., Inc.
Book Trade and Institutional Distribution by
Harper & Row

SEVENTH PRINTING

Library of Congress Catalog Card Number: 64-17106
©1964 by American Heritage Publishing Co., Inc., 551 Fifth Avenue, New York, New York, 10017. All rights reserved under Berne and Pan-American Copyright Conventions.
Trademark CARAVEL registered United States Patent Office

Though he had Viking blood, King Eric IX of Sweden ruled peaceably in the twelfth century, and even sailed with his bishops (above). The vessel is a peaceful merchantman rather than a Viking raider—a violent era was ending.

FOREWORD

Until recently the Vikings were consigned by most writers to a brutal and stormy period of history known as the Dark Ages, in which nothing of benefit to the civilized world was supposed to have happened. Against this black landscape, the Viking warriors were thought to have sprung up suddenly to commit their violent deeds, and then with equal suddenness and with no significant effect, to have disappeared.

Yet it was the Vikings who discovered America, who dominated much of Western Europe for three centuries (800–1100), and who established the first royal house of Russia. The Viking King Canute was at one point king of England and Norway as well as of his native Denmark. Viking art (many examples of which are included in this book) and Viking literature are among the brightest and most original of Europe's cultural treasures. Furthermore, the Viking spirit—a willingness to fight lustily without fear of death—is the ideal of all embattled people.

Certainly in their own time the Vikings were an irresistible and undeniable force for change. Chieftains from the Northland took advantage of the chaos in Europe to conquer fertile territories for themselves and their sons, thus creating a common Viking lineage for much of Europe's nobility. Viking traders forced open blocked trade routes for their cargoes of slaves and plunder. Viking explorers added Iceland and Greenland, and hints of lands even farther west, to world maps.

But the greatest effect of what is now called the Viking Era was on the Vikings themselves. When the era began, they were a primitive people who possessed, chiefly, pagan vitality, remarkable native ships, and hunger for riches. At the end of it they had become devout Christians, law-abiding Europeans, and early capitalists. The Swedish King Eric IX (1150–60), who centralized his government's administration and worked closely with the princes of the Church, was a whole civilization removed from Ivar the Boneless, whose bowmen executed King Edmund of East Anglia in 867.

Like one of their own tapestries, the Vikings' history is fiercely colorful, and rich with meaning.

THE EDITORS

This fleet of five wrecked Viking ships was recently found on the sea bottom near Copenhagen and is being restored by archaeologists.
COPYRIGHT ROYAL DANISH MINISTRY FOR FOREIGN AFFAIRS

COVER: *Breasting the waves of the North Atlantic, Leif Ericson's ship with its billowing square sail reached America about 1002.*
JEFFERSON PARK FIELD HOUSE, CHICAGO PARK DEPARTMENT

ENDSHEETS: *An old Viking tapestry, reconstructed here, presents a vivid pattern of processional carts and spear-bearing warriors.*
UNIVERSITETETS OLDSAKSAMLING, OSLO

TITLE PAGE: *Thor was the god of the Viking common man; his symbol was a hammer. This silver Thor's hammer has an eagle's face.*
AMERICAN SWEDISH NEWS EXCHANGE

CONTENTS

	FOREWORD	7
I	TERROR OF THE EMPIRE	10
II	RAIDERS AND PIRATES	26
III	THE GREAT INVASIONS	42
IV	VIKINGS OF THE EAST	62
V	BURIED PLUNDER	78
VI	EXPLORERS AND COLONISTS	96
VII	WINELAND THE GOOD	112
VIII	THE END OF THE VIKINGS	134
	ACKNOWLEDGMENTS	150
	FURTHER REFERENCE	151
	INDEX	152

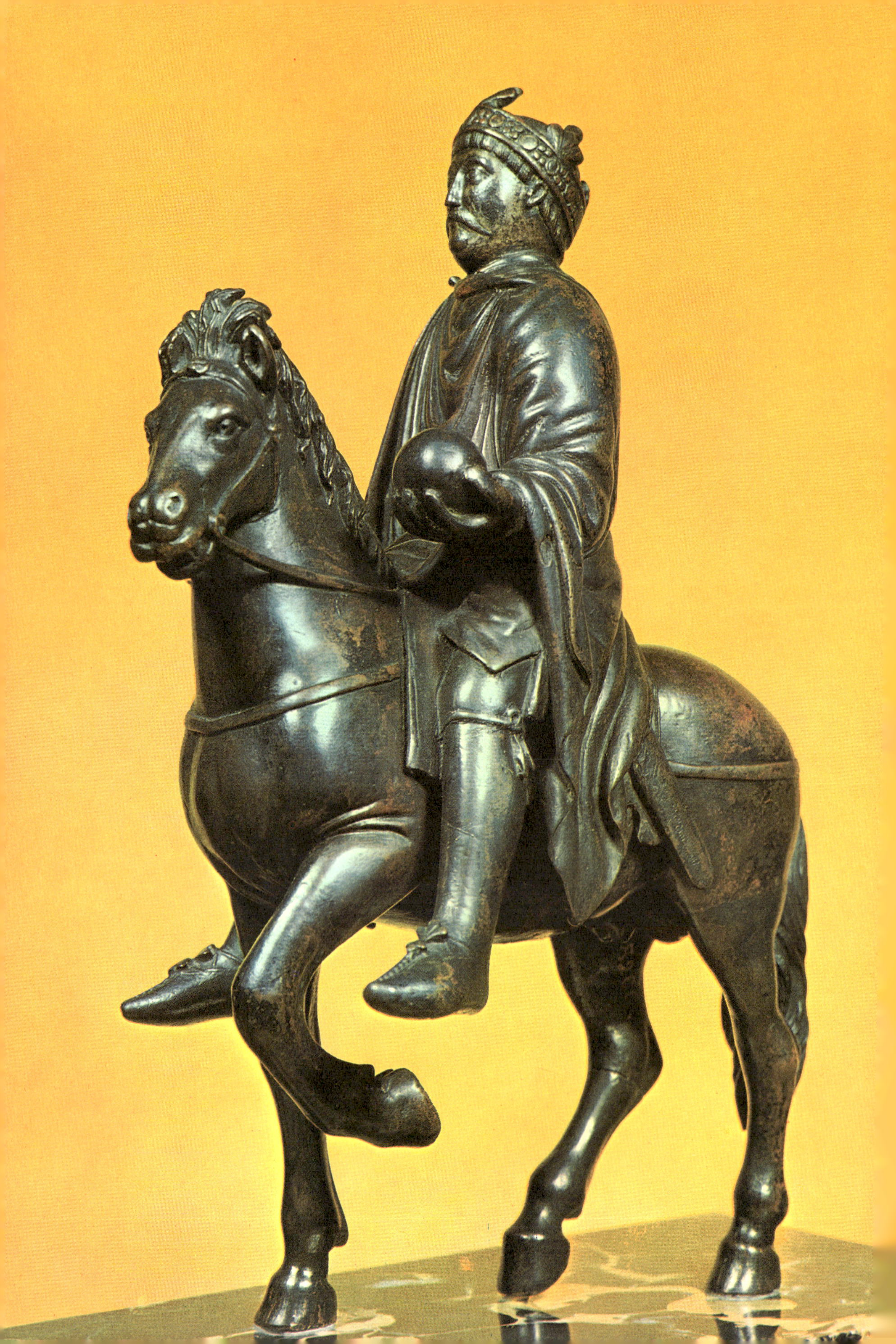

I

TERROR OF THE EMPIRE

A thousand candles blazed in the nave of St. Peter's in Rome on Christmas Day in the year 800. They glinted like tiny stars on the jewels in the crown that Pope Leo III placed on the head of the kneeling Charles. He had knelt as King of the Franks. He rose as Charlemagne (Charles the Great), Emperor of the Romans.

As Charlemagne left the splendor of Rome to ride back to the crude capital he was building at Aix-la-Chapelle (in present-day Germany near the Belgian border), he could look back over thirty-two years of riding and fighting to put the Western Roman Empire back together again under the Church of Rome. In his younger days the towering warrior had led the Frankish troops across the Alps to protect the pope from the Lombards; across the Rhine to conquer and convert the pagan Saxons; down the Danube to pursue the wild Avars; across the Pyrenees to push back the Moors in Spain—here the noble knight Roland fell. Now, as Emperor, he ruled from central Italy to the River Elbe, which formed the border between his empire and the distant Northland—Denmark and Scandinavia.

During peaceful periods Charlemagne left the saddle for the study. While his liegemen held the borders, their lord turned to the library. Only a spark of learning had been left burning in Europe since the Germanic tribes had burst upon the Roman Empire 400 years before. Charlemagne assembled scholars to renew the flame. To his palace at Aix-la-Chapelle he added a library and a school in which monks learned to copy books in the clear Carolingian script that is the basis of present writing. The oldest existing manuscripts of Caesar, Tacitus, Suetonius,

Charlemagne was emperor of much of Europe in the ninth century, when the Viking Era began. Wearing the drooping mustache of that time, he sits on his charger at left; in the tenth-century drawing above, he is enthroned.

and many of the works of Cicero were copied here. Charlemagne borrowed books from monasteries far and wide—and, according to contemporary accounts, he seldom returned them.

Oxen hauled carved marbles and mosaics across the Alps to bring Roman splendor to Charlemagne's Church. Frankish artisans copied them and became skilled workers in wood, stone, and metal. At the dawn of the ninth century a new learning and a new culture were slowly starting to brighten Charlemagne's Europe, to which Frankish knights had already brought law and order and Christian unity—and, for a few years, peace.

A monk from the famous abbey of St. Gallen in Switzerland tells a tale of Charlemagne, something that happened in the year he was crowned. The Emperor was eating peacefully in a town on the Mediterranean coast when some ships were sighted coming toward the shore. His people thought the strangers were traders, but Charles, after a glance at the ships, said they were not filled with goods but with enemies. The monk's story assumes that the enemies were Northmen (although Moorish pirates were also raiding the empire's coasts at that time), and he goes on to say:

When the Northmen heard that Charles was there, they vanished in marvelously swift flight. Rising from his table, the most just and devout Charles stood looking from the window, while his tears ran down and no one dared speak to him. Then he explained his tears to his nobles in these words: 'I do not fear that these worthless scamps will do any harm to me. No, I am sad at heart thinking that while I live they dare intrude upon this shore, and I am torn by a great sorrow foreseeing what evil they will do to my descendants.'

The tale from St. Gallen is probably based on the monk's hindsight rather than the Emperor's foresight, but Charlemagne might well have wept at the havoc these "worthless scamps" would bring to his empire.

History calls them Vikings, and they began their intrusions from the north while Charlemagne was still alive, with pin-point raids on the coast of Europe. From this simple start they eventually penetrated all of England; created and administered cities in Ireland; gained a powerful province in France; controlled Frisia, the modern Netherlands; and raided around Spain, passing into the Mediterranean to harass Italy and North Africa. In another direction they established the first Russian kingdom, challenged Constantinople, and provided a personal guard for the

In the dramatic painting at right, Charlemagne is crowned on Christmas Day, 800, in St. Peter's by Pope Leo III. Behind the Pope stand white-mitered bishops of the Church; filling the aisles behind Charlemagne is a throng of French, German, and Italian subjects. As ruler of the Roman Empire, Charlemagne tried to impose peace and order and culture on his dominions. Above, in a relief carved on his tomb, he is shown weeping over the slaughter of his helmeted and mail-shirted knights. At right above, Italian monks are putting books into a decorated cabinet; this is one of the earliest medieval pictures of a library and is reminiscent of Charlemagne's passionate interest in books, scholarship, and the law.

PHOTO MARBURG   ABBEY OF MONTE CASSINO: PHOTO F. PARISIO, NAPLES

BIBLIOTHÈQUE NATIONALE: SERVICE PHOTOGRAPHIQUE

13

England ("Brittannia") appears as a J-shaped island in the upper left corner of this tenth-century world map. Scattered above England are the isles of Scotland, and to the right of them is Denmark. The Scandinavian peninsula, home of many Vikings, is the large, jagged island above Denmark.

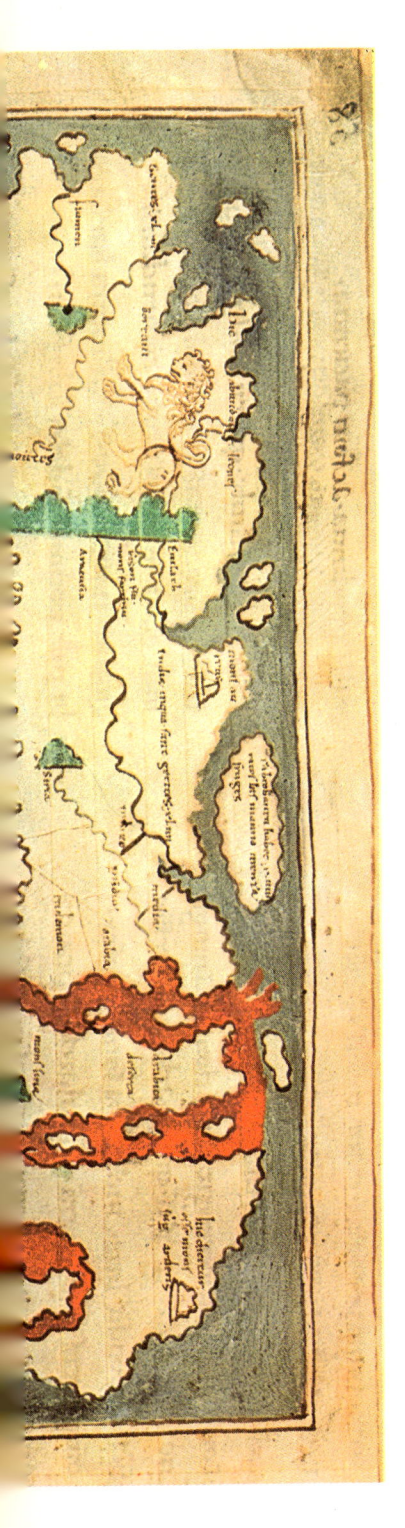

Byzantine emperor. They settled Iceland, founded a colony on Greenland, and discovered America. All of this was accomplished in the relatively short space of two and a half centuries. Then, like a flash of lightning, their historic adventures ceased.

Although the period from the end of the eighth century to the middle of the eleventh is sometimes called the Viking Era, all of the Northmen who sailed forth from their homelands during that time were not strictly Vikings. The true Viking was, to his own people, a sea-roving adventurer. Such a one was said to go *i viking*. The word itself probably comes from the Scandinavian word *vik*, meaning "bay" or "creek," and may have originally referred to raiders who lurked in inlets and bays, waiting to strike.

Those whom they visited saw nothing glamorous or romantic in the Vikings. To their victims the Northmen were plunderers, marauders, or simply pirates. The earliest chronicles describe the sudden appearance off a coast of a long, slim Viking ship with its single square sail and thirty or more oars. It swooped swiftly toward an unprotected target on an island or in a river mouth, often a monastery or an abbey. Bearded men dropped their oars, grabbed their shields, battle-axes, or double-edged swords, and swarmed ashore. They did not pause to parley. Perhaps they slew those in their path; perhaps they pushed them aside to get at the plunder. They took anything of value that would fit in their ship. If there was not enough precious metal or fine fabrics, they completed their cargo with strong young men and attractive young women to sell as slaves. If they were in an ugly mood, or found too much wine during their raid, they might apply the torch before they piled back into their ship and sailed over the horizon.

But many of the Northmen who were on the move during the Viking Era were not raiders, and never went *i viking*. Contrary to the sword-swinging tradition, some came as traders and stayed as settlers—there were Norwegian settlements in the Orkney and Shetland islands by the beginning of the ninth century. Some went exploring across the North Atlantic for new lands. Some opened trade routes across Russia to Constantinople. Some served as mercenaries and fought other invading Northmen. Indeed, the Northmen who went voyaging after the second half of the ninth century generally had a more serious purpose than hit-and-run raiding. But history labels them all as Vikings.

History does not positively explain who they were originally or why they started voyaging from their homelands

TEXT CONTINUED ON PAGE 19

STEEDS OF THE WAVES

Prior to the eighth century, Viking ships were not built for sea voyaging; nor, curiously, were they rigged for sailing. Like the famous fourth-century vessel discovered at Nydam, Denmark (a model of which appears below), the earliest ships from the Northland were usually low-sided and equipped only for rowing. The Nydam ship, although seventy-six feet long and rowed by fourteen pairs of oarsmen seated on stout thwarts, could never have sped through the cresting waves of the North Sea and landed a force of warriors hundreds of miles away. It was only in the 700's that sails began to appear on Scandinavian ships; the ships' sides were heightened, the hulls lengthened and deepened. The powerful and beautiful result was the long-distance sea raiders that Viking poets called "steeds of the waves." They flew a flag like the eagle banner at right, and the ones that served as burial vessels carried strange and grotesquely carved posts (center). An authentic relic of a Viking Era vessel, the Gokstad ship, was found near Oslo in 1881. At bottom is a scale model of the ship, with shields hung on the gunwales as if for harbor display. At far right is a rigging block that was found aboard. The Gokstad ship, though used as a tomb for a chieftain, embodied all the principles of the sea raiders: she was outfitted primarily for sailing (there were no rowers' benches), her side rudder was designed for ease in handling at sea, and the hull was built so the planks could twist slightly as the ship surged ahead. Technical advances like these allowed the Vikings to reach and strike the coasts of Europe.

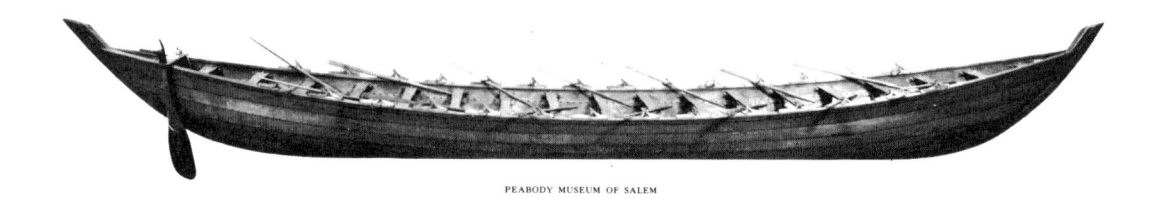

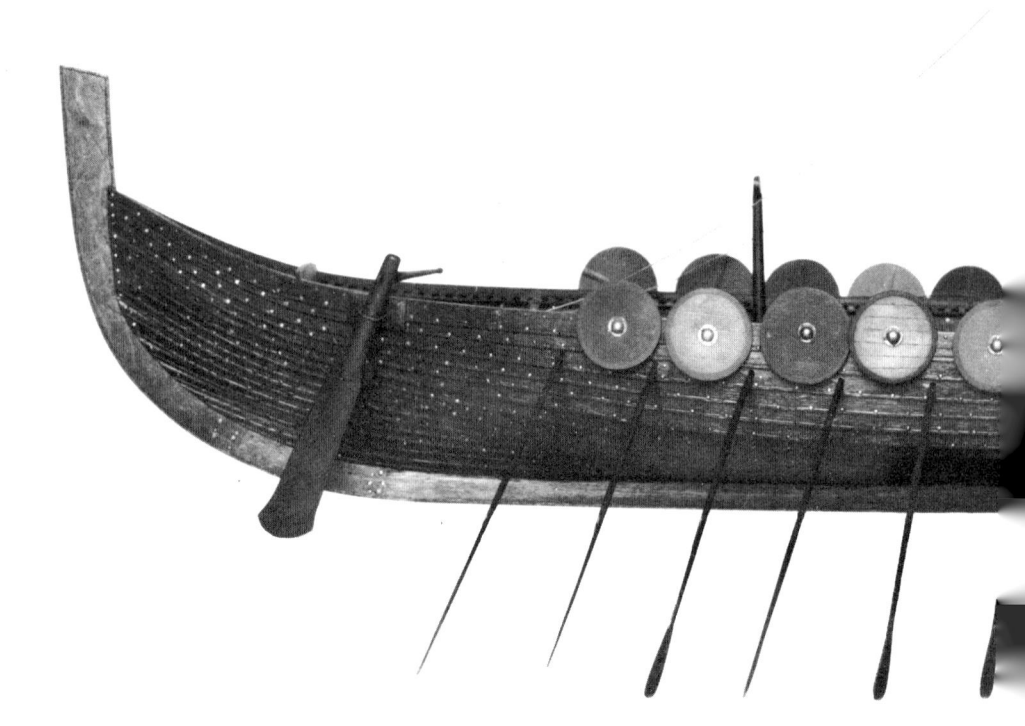

PEABODY MUSEUM OF SALEM

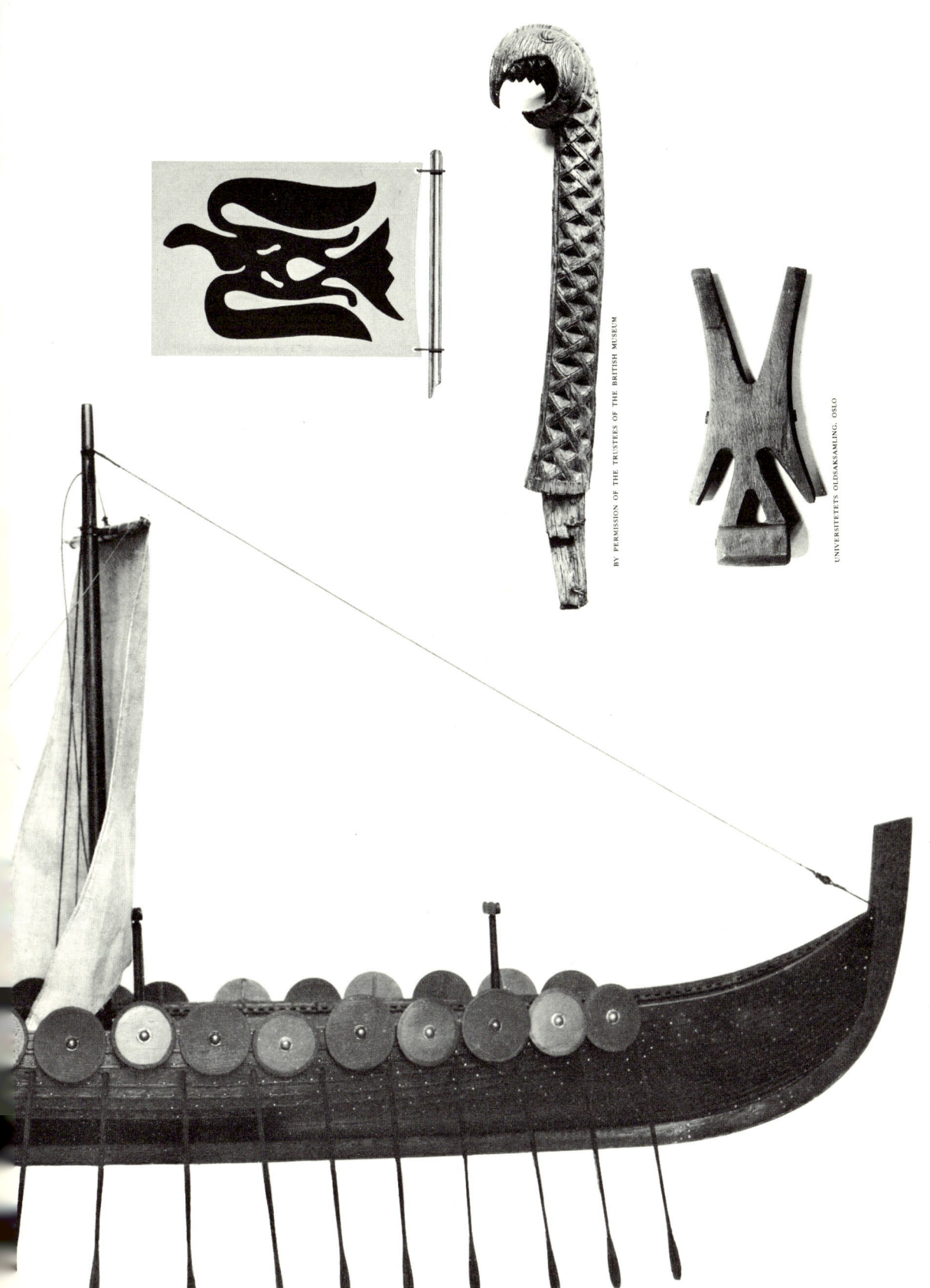

BY PERMISSION OF THE TRUSTEES OF THE BRITISH MUSEUM

UNIVERSITETETS OLDSAKSAMLING, OSLO

SMITHSONIAN INSTITUTION

A ceruice fluens tenui uelamine lembus
Concipit ingestas tetris..... tingentibus auras

equs q; pedib; soner

emin' instabili sonipes feritate superbit
Impatiens madidis frenarier ora lupatis
uc illuc frendens obuertit terga negata
flectis
ibertate fuge pressisq; timescit habenis
pretokkx
oc sese ostentans habitu nemorosa uirago
nt utraq; acie supeminet & falerum
ornatu; & ipse adequu puxx
Circuflectit equii uultu q; & uoce minii

TEXT CONTINUED FROM PAGE 15

with such dramatic suddenness; although they were undoubtedly Nordic tribes akin to the Saxons, Jutes, and Angles, who were among the first peoples to settle in England. One of the earliest Northland sagas tells of a chief named Odin who ruled a city in Asia. The story says that "the Roman emperors were going far and wide over the world, beating down all people in battle; because of the unrest many lords fled from their lands. When Odin looked into the future and worked magic, he knew that his offspring would dwell and till in the northern parts of the earth." This supposedly took place in the century before the birth of Christ. Caesar's generals were extending the Roman Empire into Asia. The story describes Odin as a man with supernatural powers, but subsequently he became the supreme Nordic god. He led his people north to rule over all whom he found there, turning himself into a bear or a wolf or a bird when necessary to serve his purposes. All the early kings of the Northmen, at the beginning of the Viking Era, claimed descent from Odin. Whether there ever was a real man at the basis of the Odin legend is uncertain, but he is still very much with us. In Old English his name was Woden; hence, Wednesday ("Woden's day"). From another god, Thor, comes Thursday, and from Odin's wife Frigg comes Friday.

There are several theories as to why the pagan Northmen suddenly exploded into Christian Europe. One is that the inhabitants of Scandinavia and Denmark had become settled, energetic folk whose farming and manufacturing (metalwork and woodwork) were nevertheless insufficient to support the number of people. Families were large, in part because a Northman could have several wives, and food was so hard to obtain that it was not uncommon for infants to be left outside to die of exposure. For individual families who began to feel the economic pinch, and particularly for younger brothers who would not inherit land, the only answer was to go *i viking*.

Another, and perhaps coincidental, theory for the beginning of the Viking movement is that the ships and the seamanship of the Northmen had advanced just at this time to the point where they could challenge the open sea. The Northmen had always been seafarers, sailing along

TEXT CONTINUED ON PAGE 22

The Viking gods were numerous and had manlike imperfections. Chief of the gods was Odin (mounted on a charger, above). Great, though cruel, he was constantly pursuing wisdom, even at the pain of death. A far lesser but better-tempered god was Frey (top), the spirit of fertility. These carvings were done before Christianity came to topple the ancient gods of the Northland.

Superior when at sea, the early Viking raiders were often outmatched on land by Frankish cavalry. The Frankish warrior at left above has slung a lion skin over his saddle and, like the knight below him, wields a battle-axe.

During the Middle Ages, intricate tapestries were woven which give a curiously two-dimensional picture of the Vikings' history. This section of such a work represents the struggle between Christianity and paganism. At the left of the tapestry, three priests ring bells to frighten away evil spirits, while another priest is at an altar inside the church. Unconcerned, birds roost on the roof.

STATENS HISTORISKA MUSEUM, STOCKHOLM

TEXT CONTINUED FROM PAGE 19

the coasts of the Northland. Now they could go anywhere.

The Northmen had raided and plundered each other across the narrow waters of their homelands before the start of the Viking Era, but relics of the older ships do not indicate that these were fast and seaworthy like the long boats with which the Vikings first invaded Europe. It may be said that many Northmen had always been temperamentally suited to go *i viking*. As soon as they developed the nautical skill and equipment to sail long distances, they sought richer and wider fields for adventure.

All of this has to be theory because the Northmen left no written records. Writing on parchment did not begin in Scandinavia and Denmark until the middle of the eleventh century, with the result that the Viking Era is like a picture that is slightly out of focus. The general pattern is clear, but the details are maddeningly blurred. What is known of the Vikings comes from three separate sources: the sagas of the Viking people themselves; the annals and chronicles of the other Europeans with whom they came in contact; and the buried relics of their existence that are now being found by archaeologists.

A castle is assaulted by sea rovers in the drawing at left, which was made toward the start of the Viking Era. Having landed in their double-ended boats, the attackers surmount the palace walls. The final stage of such an assault was the slaughter of the inhabitants (note the spears, long swords, and axes) and the freighting away of the silver, gold, and rich linens.

The sagas are stories of the exploits of the Northmen that were told around the firesides through the generations until they began to be written down in the twelfth century. It is not always possible to tell which of the sagas are meant to be historical and which are romantic fiction; and some are obviously a mixture of fiction, fact, myth, and legend. Some of the Vikings they describe were real, some were legendary. And scholars are loath to rely on the sagas after about fifteen generations of oral repetition.

The story of the Vikings was written down, as it was happening, in the ancient chronicles and annals of Ireland, England, and France. But these chronicles are not unbiased, since they were written by men who were themselves victims of the Vikings. Most of the writers were churchmen who believed that the heathen from the north were trying to destroy Christianity. To the litany of the Church in northern France was added a prayer, *A furore Normannorum libera nos Domine*—"From the fury of the Normans [Northmen], God deliver us."

The best factual evidence of the Viking Era is that unearthed by the archaeologists. Hundreds of graves have produced Viking arms and armor, as well as tools, jewelry, and coins. Before the Northmen became Christians they followed the pagan practice of burying worldly goods with the dead. Modern knowledge of Viking ships is exact and extensive because many of the vessels that were used as burial chambers ashore have been found and excavated, well preserved and nearly complete. Interesting houses, camps, and fortifications have also been uncovered.

An example of how the several sources combine to give a picture of Viking raids is the story of an attack on London. The saga of Saint Olaf tells how Olaf of Norway, at that time a roaming adventurer, helped the fugitive King Ethelred of England return to his country in 1014 and take London from its Danish captors.

The Viking leader took his ships under London Bridge and wound cables round the stakes which supported the bridge, and taking the cables, they rowed all the ships downstream as hard as ever they could. The stakes were dragged along the bottom until they were loosed under the bridge . . . and the bridge came crashing down, and many fell into the river . . . Now when the citizens saw that the River Thames was won, so that they could no longer prevent the ships from pressing up inland, they were stricken with terror at the advance of the ships and gave up the city.

Strangely, the best English record of those years, the

Legend persists that chieftains of the Vikings wore elaborate helmets rigged out with horns and wings like the one in the modern drawing above. But a Northman fortunate enough to have a helmet probably wore the conical sort seen in the medieval carving below. This warrior's helmet appears to be a leather cap reinforced with iron bands and equipped with a nosepiece of iron.

Anglo-Saxon Chronicle, does not describe this battle. It merely says that "the townsmen of London submitted and gave hostages, for they dreaded that he [Olaf] would fordo them." But in recent years several Viking battle-axes, a grappling iron, and other Viking implements have been dredged up from the bed of the Thames at the site of old London Bridge. So it is evident that such a battle did take place there, and whatever the precise date of the Viking engagement, it has been immortalized for every child in the song which begins "London Bridge is falling down, falling down, falling down . . ."

All of the non-Viking sources present the Northmen as complete villains—cruel, ruthless, vicious, bloodthirsty —slaying, pillaging, and burning all in their path. One eloquent Irish chronicler wrote:

> Although there were an hundred heads of hardened iron on one neck, and an hundred sharp, ready, cool, never rusting, brazen tongues in each head, and an hundred garrulous, loud, unceasing voices from each tongue, they could not recount or narrate or enumerate or tell what all the Gaedheal [Irish] suffered in common, both men and women, laity and clergy, old and young, noble and ignoble, of hardship and of injuring and oppressing, in every house, from those valiant, wrathful, purely pagan people.

The sagas, on the other hand, present the Vikings as brave heroes fighting against great odds. These accounts admit that the Northmen plundered. In fact, the sagas brag of it. Plundering, in ninth-century Scandinavia and Denmark, was an honorable profession, so long as it was carried on outside of home waters. The sagas glory in incidents of extreme cruelty. One favorite Viking tactic was to surround a building while the occupants were sleeping and then set fire to it, roasting some and slaughtering others as they fled from the flames.

The Vikings have been called barbarians—which they were not, although their behavior was frequently barbaric. They had a civilization and a culture of their own, with a functioning government and well-established laws. In certain democratic practices—such as community elections— they were ahead of the rest of Europe. When they were not out *i viking*, many of them were peaceful farmers. Most of the early raids were made in the spring, after the planting, and in the fall, after the harvest. Later, as the Viking bands grew bigger, they started to spend winters in the European countries, and the change-over from pirates to invaders and from invaders to settlers began to speed up.

There are, however, writers who have overstated these

Viking axes, like the one at top found in the mud of the Thames near London, were used as tools as well as weapons. They were capable of demolishing in one blow a shield like that of the beautifully robed Frankish king above.

civilizing qualities and who consider the Vikings to be consistently heroic figures. One nineteenth-century historian wrote that everything good or socially useful in European and American life can be appropriately ascribed to the Vikings. And modern film makers and fiction writers, who tend to portray the Vikings as grimacing swashbucklers, have not helped to straighten out this complimentary but distorted picture.

It is surely false to regard the Vikings as the source of all that is brutal or beautiful in the world today. Yet the Viking movement did make many noteworthy contributions to European civilization. Outstanding among them are the ideals of loyalty, courage, and individual freedom, which are shared by Viking descendants in many lands.

Pirates the Vikings were, but farmers too. Their homelands, though originally extensive and fertile, had by the ninth century become too cramped for the large population. Seeking new lands to till, the Vikings looked to the east, south, and west. Farming scenes in contemporary Italy are portrayed in the manuscript illumination above.

II

RAIDERS AND PIRATES

"Whilst the pious King Bertric was reigning over the western parts of the English, and the innocent people, spread through their plains, were enjoying themselves in tranquility and yoking their oxen to the plough, suddenly there arrived on the coast a fleet of Danes, not large, but of three ships only. This was their first arrival. When this became known, the king's officer leaped on his horse and rode with a few men to the port, thinking that they were merchants and not enemies. Giving his commands as one that had authority, he ordered them to be sent to the king's town; but they slew him on the spot and all who were with him. The name of this officer was Beaduheard."

The round Viking shield was made of wood, with a central metal knob.

So Beaduheard, overseer of King Bertric, gained a place in history as the first Viking victim. For this raid on England's south coast was the earliest attack recorded by any of the chronicles. Some sources give the date as A.D. 787, others say 789. It does not matter—nor does the reference to the raiders as Danes. The English chronicles called all Vikings Danes, the French called them Normans. Only the Irish seemed able to distinguish between visitors from Norway and Denmark, calling the former white foreigners and the latter black foreigners, perhaps because the Danes were less often blond than the Norwegians. This early raid was quickly followed by others. In 793 the Vikings sacked their first monastery, at Lindisfarne off the coast of Northumbria in England. Abbeys in the north of England, Scotland, and on the Isle of Man were the next targets.

The key to the uniform success of the early Viking raids is that nobody came to help "pious King Bertric," or any of the other petty chieftains who called themselves kings, when the Vikings struck in the small area over which each king ruled. There was no kingdom of England as such. The land was divided into minor kingdoms—Northumbria, Mercia, Wessex, Essex, Surrey, Kent, and East Anglia. The rulers of these little states were usually fighting among

An early English battle scene shows a king fighting in the midst of warriors who are armed with round Viking shields and enormous battle swords.

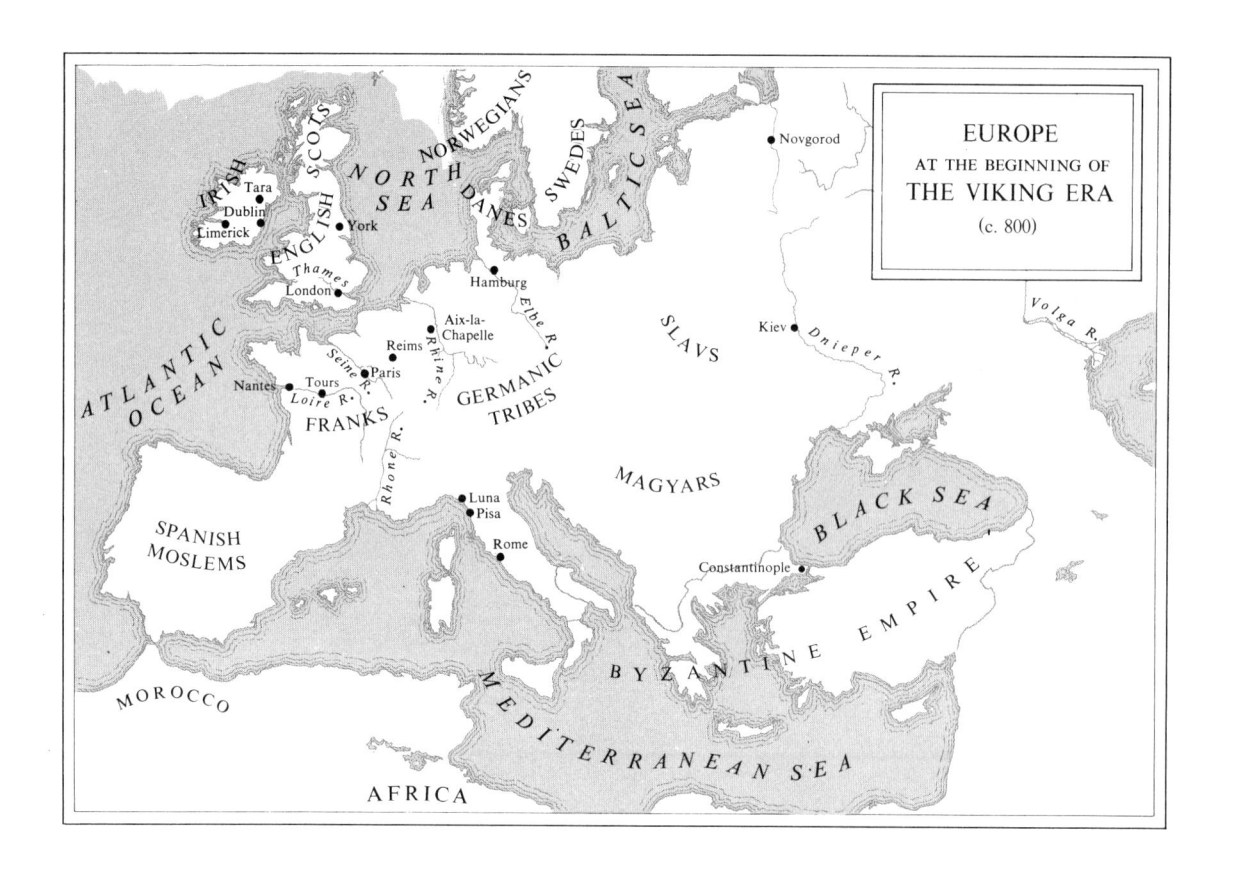

themselves and gave no thought to uniting against the Viking raiders. In fact, a Viking raid on one's next door neighbor could be cause for rejoicing. It might weaken him and make him easier prey for conquest after the raiders had gone.

After the initial raids on England, marauding Vikings began to attack the coast of nearby Ireland, a country even less capable of united resistance. Although there was a so-called high king in Ireland, he actually had no authority over the scores of petty local kings except such as he could enforce with the sword. And, just as the English kings fought each other frequently, so were the local Irish chieftains constantly at one another's throats. This situation was made to order for the Northmen. They intensified their attacks on Ireland, and that unhappy land felt the whole wrath of the Viking raiders during the first part of the ninth century. Every year the keeper of the ancient annals of Ireland entered on the list such items as "The Age of Christ, 819. The plundering of Edar by the foreigners, who carried off a great prey of women. The plundering of Beg-Eire by them also." The first attacks were sudden, swooping, hit-and-run raids by a few ships for plunder on undefended places. Monks and peasants could offer no resistance to these rough, burly pagans. The lucky Irishmen fled; the rest were slaughtered—except for those who, like the "prey of women," sailed off into slavery.

In 839 the first of the great Viking chieftains made his appearance, leading "great sea-cast floods of foreigners into Eire, so that there was not a point thereof without a fleet." Turgeis was his name, and he came not only to plunder but to conquer and rule. He first marched inland to lay waste Ireland's principal religious center at Armagh, where a bishop named Forannan was the "chief heir of Saint Patrick." This ill-starred cleric fled south, clutching

The Danes were the first Northmen to attack England. In the manuscript illumination at right, a well-ordered force of Danes storms the gate and scales the ramparts of an English town, possibly Thetford. The Danes are erroneously shown by the twelfth-century artist as being shoeless and having pointed shields. On the map at left, the Thetford raid and many other Viking strikes on England, Ireland, and Europe are indicated. Few cities had strong enough defenses to resist the Viking onslaughts.

For perhaps a thousand years before the Viking Era, the seat of Ireland's high kings was at Tara. In this photograph of Tara's site a large circular ridge that encompasses two smaller interlocked circles can be seen. The ridge marks the ramparts of the Fort of Kings, which once protected the palaces within. Despite Tara's imposing appearance, no high king was strong enough to muster unified resistance against the early Viking attacks.

relics of Ireland's patron saint, only to fall into the hands of another Viking band near Limerick.

Turgeis raged through northern Ireland, plundering churches in town after town. He placed his wife, Ota, in control of the ancient Celtic monastery of Clonmacnoise, and she, a pagan priestess, made wild prophecies in the manner of the Greek oracles from the high altar. There were many pitched battles, of which the Vikings lost a few. But Turgeis' forces were constantly being increased by fresh sea-borne bands, and the Irish kings were still more interested in fighting one another than in joining together to stave off the Vikings.

The Vikings were probably the first mailed warriors the Irish had ever seen; the men of Eire had no armor. In describing one battle, the annals say that the Irish troops "had nothing to protect their bodies and necks and gentle heads save only elegant tunics with smooth fringes and shields and beautiful finely wrought collars." The Vikings in the same fight are described as forming "a solid, skillful, and firm rampart of strong coats of mail like a thick, dark stronghold of black iron, with a green polished wall of battle shields around their chiefs."

By the year 840 Turgeis ruled all of northern Ireland, and the Vikings had established fortified bases which would become some of Ireland's principal cities. The present Castle of Dublin is said to be atop the original Viking fort, and Turgeis styled himself King of Dublin until he was captured by the Irish and drowned in a lake. One early writer tells a more romantic story of his death. In this version Turgeis was beguiled by a beautiful Irish princess to an amorous tryst on an island in Lake Owel. When the Viking king arrived, the handmaidens of the princess doffed their female attire to disclose fifteen brawny Irishmen who threw Turgeis in the lake and held him under until he drowned. The beautiful princess and her "maidens" probably stem from the Irish love of a good story. The ancient annals merely say that Turgeis was drowned

The Irish were fiercely devoted to their land and its ancient traditions. One of the customs noted by a Welshman who visited Ireland in the twelfth century was the coronation of a king by a strange rite in which the new king bathed in a broth of horsemeat while he and his attendants ate the meat (below). According to this visitor, Irish soldiers were usually armed only with axes (whether on foot or pickaback, bottom left), and the harp (bottom right) was the instrument most often heard in Tara's halls.

in "the Age of Christ, 845 . . . through the miracle of God and the saints in general."

The Vikings in Ireland, though deprived of Turgeis' leadership, were united in 853 under Olaf the White of Norway, who reigned for eighteen years and became such an important figure that after expeditions against Vikings in Scotland and England, he was given the grand title of King of the Northmen and of all Ireland and Britain. In his reign Ireland also became a vital trading nation; the various Irish kings maintained their positions by cooperating with or defending themselves against the Viking overlord in Dublin. There emerged a class known as the *Gaill-Gaedhil*, Irishmen who adopted the Viking way of life.

Meanwhile, the Vikings had avoided Charlemagne's well-defended empire except for sporadic raids. The final fight of his battle-scarred life was with the Danes in 810, but this was a small war rather than a raid. Nearing seventy, the grizzled Emperor mounted his charger for the last time and led the Frankish troops against Godfred of Denmark, who had established himself on the coast of Frisia and incited the local tribes to revolt. Just as Charlemagne's host approached, a disgruntled soldier

Charlemagne's son, Louis the Pious, was not a warrior like his father, but he was able to keep the Viking raiders from the empire's coast. He was so fearful of the Vikings that when ambassadors from Constantinople came to him in 839 accompanied by two tall, blond men, he imprisoned them because they looked like Vikings and might be spies. At left the ambassadors point out to Louis that these strangers should be released since they are really Russians of Viking descent.

stabbed Godfred to death, and the leaderless Danes went home. Charlemagne punished the local offenders with his usual severity, built a string of fortifications along the River Elbe, and ordered armed vessels to patrol the harbors of his domain to counter Viking raids. Then, in 814, he died.

He was succeeded by his son Louis the Pious, a devout, studious man who was more interested in reading the Latin classics than in fighting with anybody. But the empire was still united, and although Charlemagne's naval patrol was neglected, the Vikings avoided the coast. Louis' major contact with the Northmen was the conversion of Harold of Denmark to Christianity. Harold wanted Frankish help to gain the Danish throne. He sailed up the Rhine to Mainz and offered himself, his family, and his followers as converts. The delighted Louis personally baptized Harold, Louis' wife did the same for Harold's wife, and his son Lothair for Harold's son Godfred. Then Harold sailed home with two missionaries. He never attained the Danish throne, but Christianity gained a toe hold in the Northland.

Louis the Pious died in 840, and the empire was split up among his three sons, Louis the German, Lothair, and Charles the Bald. The united empire of Charlemagne was no more—and the way was opened for the Vikings to prey upon the land while the three kings and the local dukes struggled among themselves for power.

The slim Viking vessels swooped down on the divided empire like flocks of ravenous birds, whose images flapped overhead on the Vikings' banners. For the remainder of the century there was seldom a time when one or more bands were not storming through the land. The bands were bigger now and bolder, plundering entire cities as well as churches. Their raids were favored by the geography of what is now called France. The land was watered by many navigable rivers; most of the principal cities were on waterways. The Vikings could sail or row to the doorsteps of their victims. The sack of Nantes is typical of the fate that befell many cities in France, Germany, and the Low Countries.

The town, held by a Frankish force for Charles the Bald, was being besieged by rebels on the land side. Frankish sources tell that the rebels had invited a Viking fleet recently arrived at the mouth of the Loire to sail inland and attack Nantes from the river. Whether this was so or not, on St. John's Day, 843, a fleet of sixty-seven ships did sail up the Loire and approach the town's undefended riverbank. Apparently the ships were unobserved until

TEXT CONTINUED ON PAGE 36

This sculpture of Louis the Pious was done in the thirteenth century.

OVERLEAF: *An eleventh-century artist painted this besieged city and put himself in the picture—bottom right. Armed forces (with knobbed shields) have surrounded the pallisaded city and are ready to storm it from two directions.*

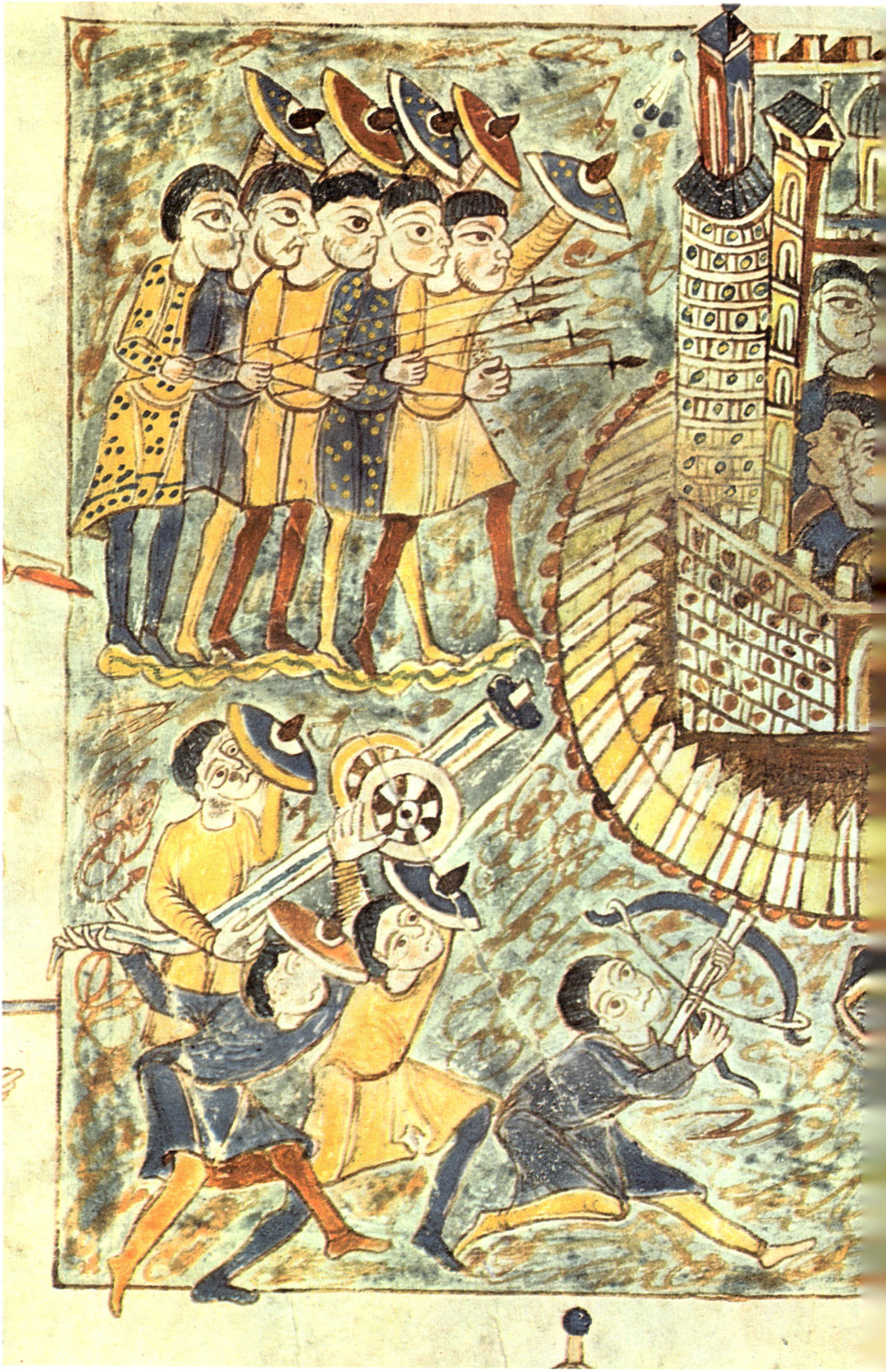

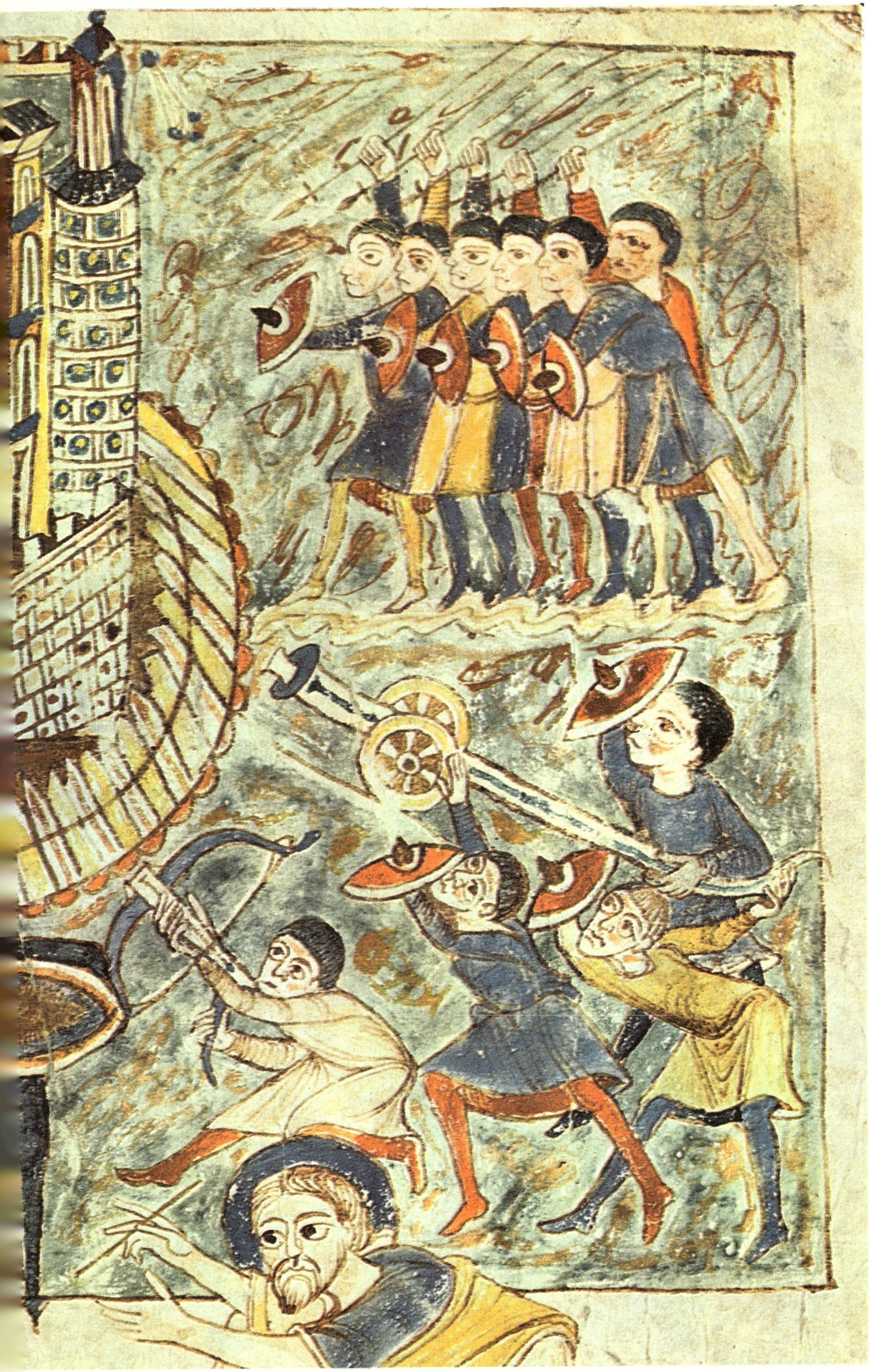

TEXT CONTINUED FROM PAGE 33

hundreds of Vikings poured ashore. The account in the Frankish chronicle is probably exaggerated, but it describes the invaders cutting down everyone they met in the streets. They broke into houses, pulled out all valuables, and fired the buildings. The cathedral was thronged when they burst in to butcher the congregation in the pews, hack down the bishop at the altar, strip and then fire the building. When night fell, they returned to their vessels, herding those whom they had selected as slaves before them through the burning city. With their booty aboard their ships, they dropped down the river.

But this band did not go home. They stayed for the winter on the island of Noirmoutier near the mouth of the Loire, which they had first looted and then fortified. This marked a new phase of Viking tactics that quickly spread to other rivers. From that time on, there were permanent advance posts at several river mouths. Various bands came and went, and slaves and plunder were shipped out to Ireland or the homeland.

Also, some raids took on a different tactical character. The Vikings would land, usually on an island well up in a river, and scour the countryside for horses. Then, with two thirds of their men mounted and the rest left behind to guard the ships, they would go on an extended foray, hitting town after town until they had worked their way back to their temporary base, laden with loot. If they had to fight, they fought dismounted; the Vikings did not use their horses in battle as did the Frankish knights. But the Vikings would avoid battle if possible. They were there for plunder, not for conquest.

Despite the lack of united resistance among their opponents, it seems incredible that the Vikings could maintain themselves year after year in an enemy country where they were so greatly outnumbered. Any estimate of how many Vikings were striking at the empire is little better than a guess. Some of the old chronicles tell of armies of forty thousand men, but this is probably a great exaggeration, at least during the first century of the Viking Era. These were private bands, not national armies. It is probable that most numbered in the hundreds rather than the thousands. True, bands joined together for a particular enterprise; a group of them came to be known as the Seine Vikings, for they always pillaged along that river. But it is unlikely that they ever put more than a few thousand in the field at a time, and they ravaged a land whose potential defenders were in the hundreds of thousands.

A Viking's most prized weapon was his sword, often inlaid and beautifully carved. This sword hilt is made of iron, copper, and silver.

Besides disunity in the empire, another reason for the Vikings' success was that they were all seasoned fighting men; few of their enemies were. Kings and dukes did not maintain standing armies, other than small personal bodyguards. When Charles the Bald called out his men to face the Vikings, most of those who responded were farm workers, without armor, untrained, and poorly armed. Only the nobles and their few household troops—housecarls—were a match for the Vikings in arms and armor. And, most important, the Vikings had complete control of the sea. If an attack was not going well, they could withdraw and escape in their ships to strike at some weaker point.

All records indicate that the Vikings excelled their enemies in strategy and tactics. The concept that they were wild, brainless brutes is wrong; archaeological finds indicate, for example, that playing chess was a favorite pastime. And the Northmen had complicated battle formations, the favorite of which seems to have been based on a wedge or triangle. Each leader was the point of a wedge and was covered by his shieldman. Other fighters were formed fanlike behind the point, each man armed with a long spear and an axe or a sword. Several of these wedges might be placed side-by-side, touching at the bases. Behind them slingers, javelin throwers, and archers were arrayed in lines, and in addition there were rows of replacements for men in the wedges.

One of the Vikings' favorite tactics was to feign a disorganized retreat, in order to draw opponents out of formation, and then rapidly regroup and turn on their pursuers. This could be done only by highly disciplined troops. Although the Vikings were fiercely independent and stressed the equality of the individual, they maintained iron discipline in combat and gave implicit obedience to a chosen leader.

As individual fighters the Northmen probably excelled most of their opponents; weaklings did not go *i viking*. Although they would retreat strategically, to turn tail from fear was inconceivable. There was no greater honor than to die in battle; in their pagan faith, a worthy hero would be carried by the Valkyries, maidens who served Odin, to eternal bliss in Valhalla. The sagas tell of dying Vikings chanting a list of their brave deeds, perhaps so that the Valkyries would know that here were deserving passengers for their heaven-bound steeds.

The sagas also tell of the berserkers. These were mighty champions who developed a fanatical rage when facing an

Chess was one of the Viking games. This chessman, a mounted Viking carved out of walrus ivory, was found in Scotland's western isles.

STRUTT, *A Complete View of the Dress...*, 1842

Viking costumes made by the artistic weavers of the Northland were strikingly colorful. At left is a nineteenth-century engraving that attempts to show the bright Viking dress and weapons. Still visible on a Viking sword (below, left) found in the Thames River is the decorative work on the pommel and the hilt. Strong patterns and vibrant colors characterize Viking craftwork, especially crisscrossed and checkered designs. Thus the bearded sea rovers depicted on the stone carving at right wear plaid shirts (possibly mail) and pull on the lines of their checkered sail.

enemy, and in this condition, had superhuman strength. They threw away their shields and cast off their shirts of mail and mowed down all before them with sword, axe, or club. There is one tale of a man who had twelve sons:

They were all great berserkers. They went on warfare when they were quite young and ravaged far and wide, but met with no equal in strength and courage.... It was their custom, if they were with only their own men when they found the *berserks gang* [berserk fury] coming over them, to go ashore and wrestle with large stones or trees, otherwise in their rage they would have slain their friends.

The greatest of the Viking leaders of the ninth century was the Dane Ragnar Lodbrok, who crops up in so many places and over such a long period of time that all of the stories about him cannot be true. Legend tells how he got the name Lodbrok and a wife, Thora, at the same time. Thora was a Swedish princess whom no man had wed because her castle was surrounded by a ditch infested with gigantic and deadly poisonous adders. Ragnar prepared to cross the moat by dressing in skins, hair side out. He then coated his costume with pitch as proof against adder bites. Hence the nickname Lodbrok—"hairy britches."

The sagas record that Ragnar was in Finland, Russia, and the Hellespont. They place him in Ireland shortly

STATENS HISTORISKA MUSEUM, STOCKHOLM: A.T.A.

39

When a Viking fleet sailed south to Spain, the Northmen came upon Moors for the first time. These ferocious warriors, who resembled the noisy band of horsemen in the Spanish miniature below, were as effective as the Vikings in ruining the last of the Roman Empire. By 800 they had conquered most of Spain and, with other Moslems, destroyed Europe's overseas trade.

after Turgeis. Ragnar sailed up the Loire to sack Nantes and Tours, and he fought on the Garonne River at the destruction of Bordeaux and Toulouse. His greatest raid was an attack on Paris with 120 ships. After lengthy fighting, he took much booty and many prisoners, but before he could capture the city, a heavy mist descended. After the mist cleared, a sickness beset the Viking host and persisted until they gave up their prisoners and loot—Christian chroniclers called the sickness an act of God.

Ragnar supposedly had many sons, of whom two had the interesting names of Ivar the Boneless and Bjorn Ironside. The far-ranging Viking exploits of Ragnar's sons are better authenticated than those of their father, particularly the longest of all Viking raids, which was led by Bjorn Ironside and another leader named Hastings in 859. This brought them into combat with the Moors around the Mediterranean, where the recording of history was far more advanced than in Europe. Moorish historians who described the Viking activity in the Mediterranean called them *Madjus*, meaning "barbarian wizards."

Bjorn and Hastings started off from the Seine in 859 with sixty-two ships. They sailed through the Bay of Biscay and landed on the northern coast of Spain—where they received an unpleasant surprise. The defenders of the Spanish peninsula were not squabbling among themselves. The Moslem Moors who conquered Spain were a tough, disciplined, unified fighting force, and they quickly drove the Vikings back to their ships. Sailing on through the Strait of Gibraltar, the Vikings fought a naval battle with a Moorish fleet, and after burning the mosque in the town of Algeciras, crossed over to Morocco. Here, says one Moorish account, "the *Madjus*—God curse them—landed at Nekor . . . plundered it, and made its inhabitants slaves, except those who saved themselves by flight."

From Morocco the raiders recrossed the Mediterranean and took up winter quarters on an island in the mouth of the Rhone River. From here they plundered the Rhone Valley at will. Then in the year 860, according to a lively, but dubious, contemporary account, the Viking band turned into northern Italy and set out on their most ambitious project, the sack of Rome.

They first plundered Pisa and then approached the city of Luna, which they are said to have mistaken for Rome. Luna was too strongly fortified for direct attack, so they asked for a truce and sent in word that one of their leaders was sick and wanted to die a Christian. Obliging clergy came out and baptized Hastings. Next day came word that the new convert had died. Could the Vikings bury him in consecrated ground within the city? The gates were opened for the funeral procession. When enough mourners were within to hold the gates, Hastings rose from his coffin, sword in hand, and the main body of Vikings rushed in.

For the first three quarters of the ninth century the Vikings were almost invariably successful everywhere they struck except in Spain. Europe no longer had a leader strong enough to unite the provincial kings and lords in order to resist the Northmen. Had they been bent on conquest instead of plunder, they might readily have become the rulers of most of Western Europe.

Over three thousand stones with runic writing and symbols have been found in the Northland. This rune stone, which may tell a story as complex as that of Hastings' journey, is carved in the Viking manner. Within an elaborate border are two picture panels: the lower one shows a Viking ship making a long sea voyage (note the cresting waves); in the upper one a chieftain rides a fast-stepping horse.

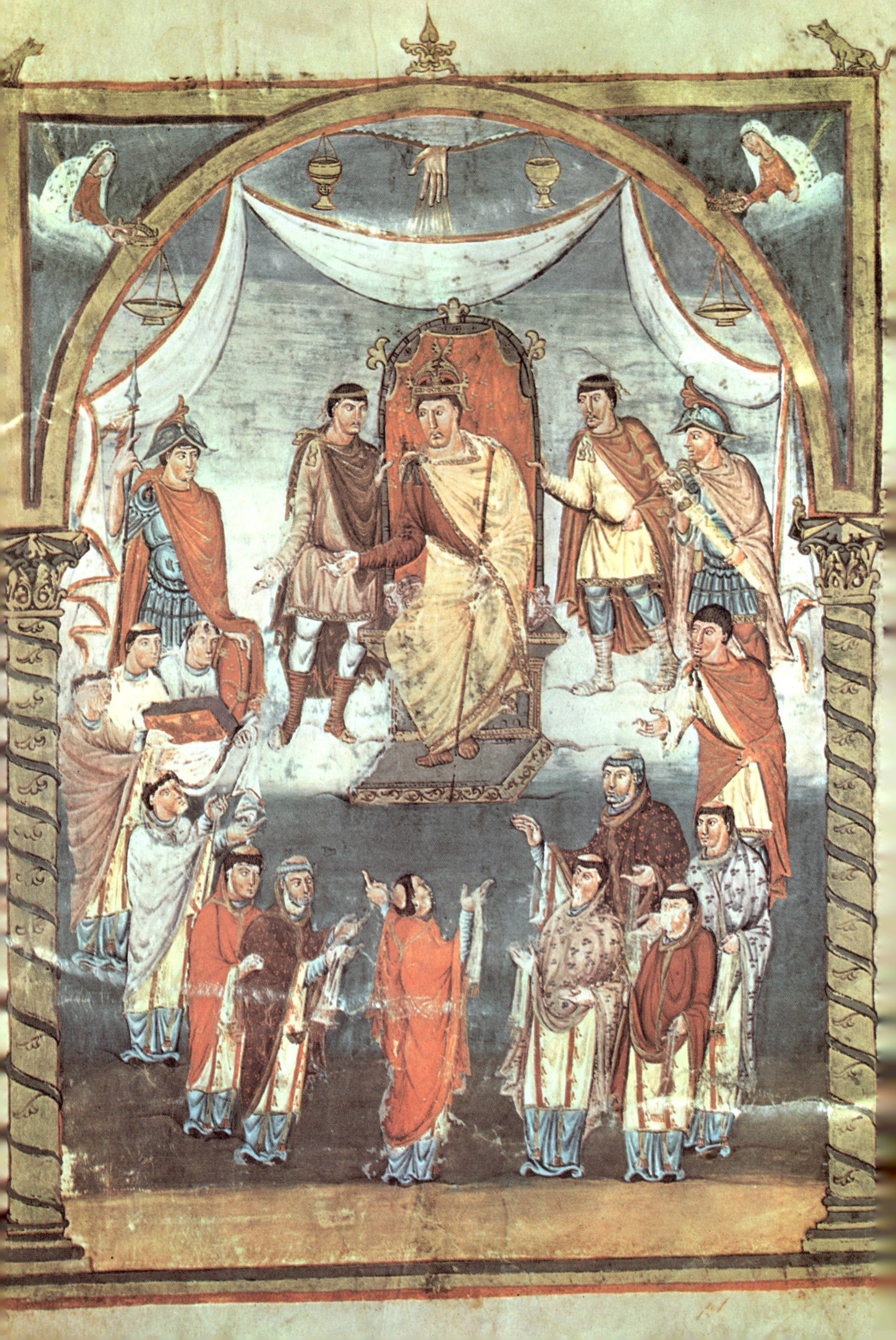

III

THE GREAT INVASIONS

One of the most famous stories in English history tells of the king dressed as a hunter who entered a peasant cottage and asked for shelter. The old woman who lived there did not recognize him, but she let him sit by the fire and told him to watch the cakes that were baking. When she returned, the cakes were burned, and she upbraided the king unmercifully. The old woman and the cakes were probably legendary, but the king was not. He is known to history as King Alfred the Great of England. The year was 878—and if the young monarch did let the cakes burn, it was surely because he was wondering what to do about the Vikings who had driven him to hiding in a swamp with a handful of followers. It seemed unlikely then that this slight, sickly young man would become the first strong leader of Europe to curb the Viking menace.

The Northmen had by this time become established in Ireland, and their attacks on the Frankish kingdom were unfailingly successful. Nothing seemed to stand in the way of their terrorization of all Europe—neither the minor kings of England, who now began to see that the Vikings were intent on permanent possession of their land, nor Charles the Bald, the king of the West Franks. Charles had begun his reign hoping to equal his grandfather, Charlemagne, in power, but he had been reduced to bribing the Viking invaders to depart after taking what they wanted.

Early in the reign of Charles the Bald—toward the middle of the ninth century—the nature of the Viking raids began to change. The cruelest evidence of this change was a military force the Danish Vikings gathered for the invasion of England. Historians refer to this force as the Great Army, and it was indeed wholly different, both in size

Viking Era monarchs had to fight as well as rule. At left are Charles the Bald and his ministers; above are Viking chess figures of a king and queen.

When the Danish Vikings captured East Anglia in 870, they introduced the worship of their gods. But King Edmund refused to accept pagan leadership. According to an oft-told legend, which this illumination illustrates, he was pulled from his throne by the Vikings and killed. A generation later, the site of the martyr's tomb became a vital Christian center; the town of Bury St. Edmunds stands there now.

and in purpose, from the raiding bands of earlier years.

General of the Great Army was the wily Ivar the Boneless, whose nickname allegedly referred to an accident of birth that gave gristle instead of bones to his body. Landing in the kingdom of East Anglia in the fall of 865, the army spent the winter planning its campaign strategy and gathering horses. When spring came, the Vikings suddenly advanced northward, seized York in Northumbria, and succeeded in holding the city against a vain attempt to relieve it in 867.

With the establishment of a foothold in Northumbria by Ivar the Boneless, the Northmen had come to England to stay. Probing and plundering farther inland, Ivar's well-disciplined horsemen knifed into the weakly ruled kingdoms of England. In East Anglia, where the Viking forces had first landed, King Edmund fought valiantly but fruitlessly. He was finally captured and deposed, and apparently declined to serve the Vikings in any capacity. Legend has it that when Edmund refused to become the vassal of a pagan, Ivar had him bound to a tree and Vikings shot arrows into him until he died. The martyrdom of King Edmund—now revered as Saint Edmund—is one of the most widely known stories of Viking atrocity. In England today many churches bear the name of this saint who became a symbol of English resistance.

After the submission of East Anglia, the Vikings controlled all the eastern plain of England. In January of 871 they descended on Wessex, hoping to destroy English arms entirely. But in the hills near Ashdown they were met by the staunch resistance of troops gathered by King Ethelred and his twenty-two-year-old brother Alfred. Fired by Alfred's daring command, the English were victorious at Ashdown and went on to fight the Vikings in nine pitched battles during the following year. When Ethelred died, Alfred's accession to the throne of Wessex was greeted with acclaim.

He was a sensitive and scholarly young man, but he was

One of England's most treasured relics is a ninth-century ornament two and a half inches long known as the Alfred Jewel. Around its outer rim is the inscription "Alfred ordered me to be made." The rim, which terminates in a boar's head, encircles an enamel portrait of a king holding crossed scepters.

also a determined and shrewd general and a king who had the welfare of his subjects at heart—something unique in ninth-century England. The people and the minor nobles, through love and respect, readily united behind him against the Viking invaders. Alfred and his soldiers met each new assault with all the force they could muster, but the struggle was an unequal one. Outnumbered, and seeing his troops weakened and weary, Alfred made an offer of peace, as so many other kings of England and Europe before him had done. He paid the invaders tribute, or Danegeld, with the stipulation that they withdraw from Wessex.

Then in the spring of 876 a new Viking chief, Halfdan, struck again. His men marched into Wessex, ravaging the countryside and battling ceaselessly with Alfred's soldiers. But the king of Wessex held on stubbornly, and the Vikings were forced to withdraw to the north where their holdings were uncontested.

The low point in Alfred's reign was in 878, when a third Viking leader, Guthrum, swooped into Wessex to surprise Alfred's court during the Christmas celebration. The attack was so unexpected and so fierce that the morale of the people of Wessex gave way. They fled from the Vikings, their king taking refuge in the marshes of Somerset—it was

Alfred is considered the first English king to have the vision of a united nation. In this charming but inaccurate nineteenth-century engraving, the aged ruler leans on the shoulder of his great-grandson Edgar (who was, in fact, born long after Alfred died). Edgar came to the throne in 959, when Viking warriors had temporarily withdrawn; thus, he was the first king to be recognized as ruler of all England.

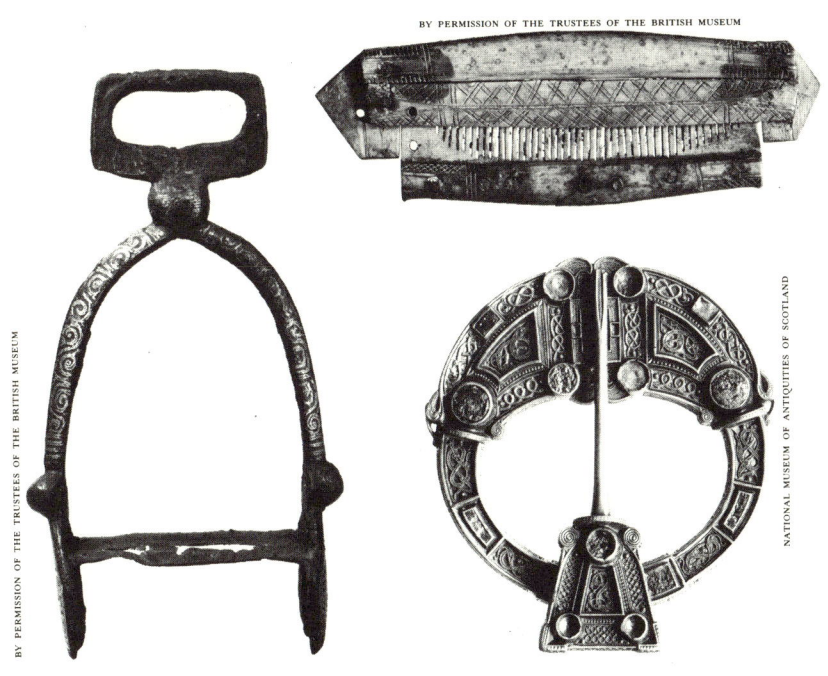

The Vikings who occupied much of the British Isles liked hardware and ornaments that were highly decorative but rugged. Between the intricately carved and inlaid stirrup and sword hilt above are two pieces of finery owned by Viking ladies. The beautifully wrought comb was originally Celtic; the silver brooch was found in York.

here Alfred is supposed to have allowed the cakes to burn.

But Alfred was not beaten. Refugees came to join him to form a tiny army. He built a stockaded fort on an island in the marshes—the only point in England that was holding out against the Vikings. From this island Alfred sallied forth during the spring to keep the Northmen off balance with guerrilla tactics while he sent messages through the countryside to rally support. By Easter he had gathered sufficient forces to attack. Now it was the Vikings' turn to suffer from a surprise assault. Alfred drove them into their armed camp and there starved them into submission. Guthrum and the principal leaders agreed to become Christians and never again to set foot in Wessex. The peace treaty that followed Alfred's victory divided England into two distinct areas: to the north and east was the Danelaw —that territory in which Danish laws and customs were in effect; and to the south and west were Alfred's possessions, which included much of Mercia. But the important result of the treaty was that under Alfred the south of England was united in spirit; it would be united in fact when Alfred liberated London from the Danes in 886.

Even though the Danelaw became more peaceable, Alfred's kingdom was never completely free from Viking attacks throughout the remainder of his reign. He built a fleet of vessels larger than those of the Vikings and gained the title, in some histories, of Father of the British Navy.

TEXT CONTINUED ON PAGE 51

This modern mural dramatizes the victory of Alfred's large, lion-headed ships (background) over the smaller Viki

...ips at the Battle of Swanage Bay in 877. Violent winds also played a part in this naval setback for the Vikings.

BY PERMISSION OF THE TRUSTEES OF THE BRITISH MUSEUM

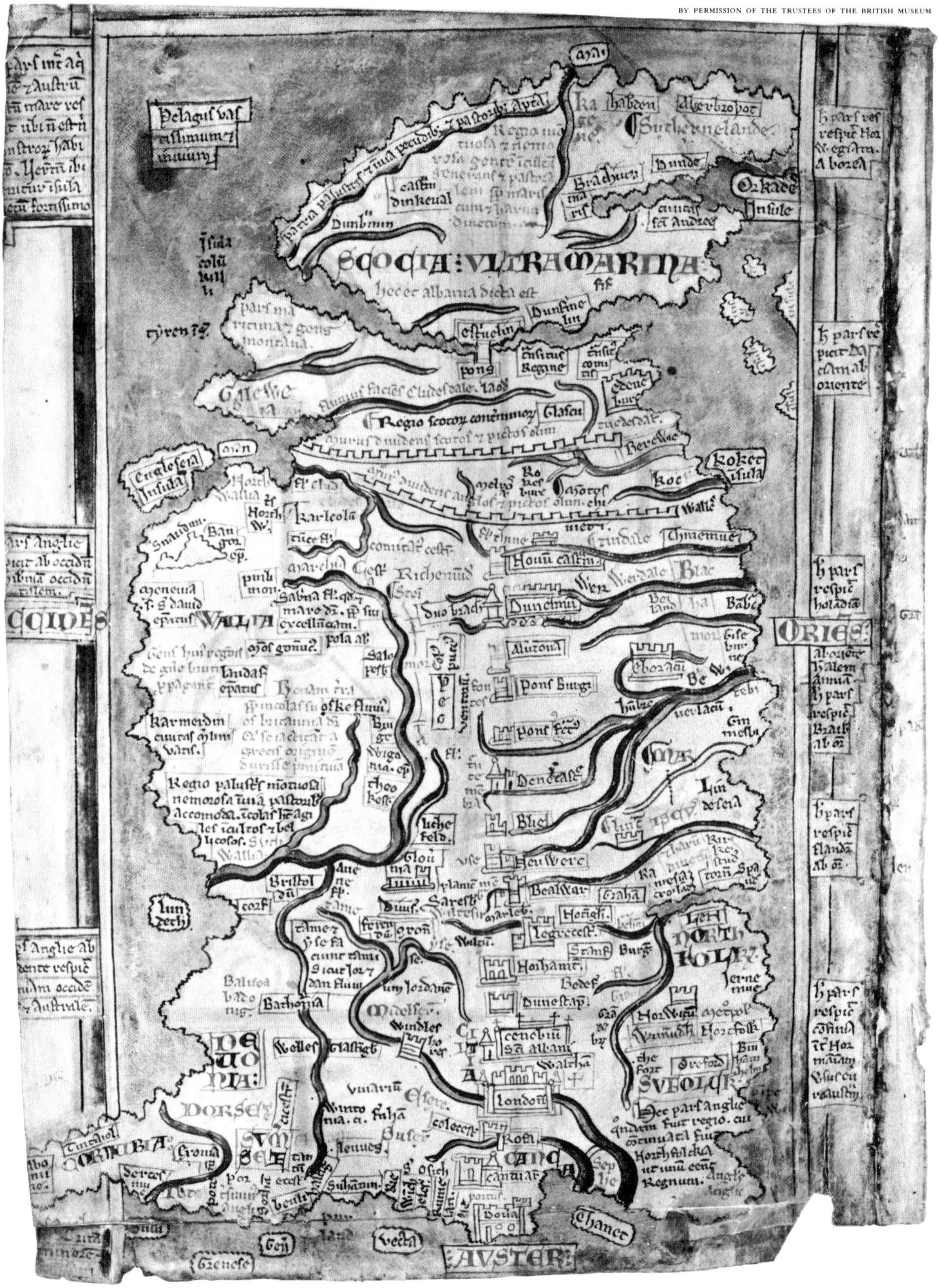

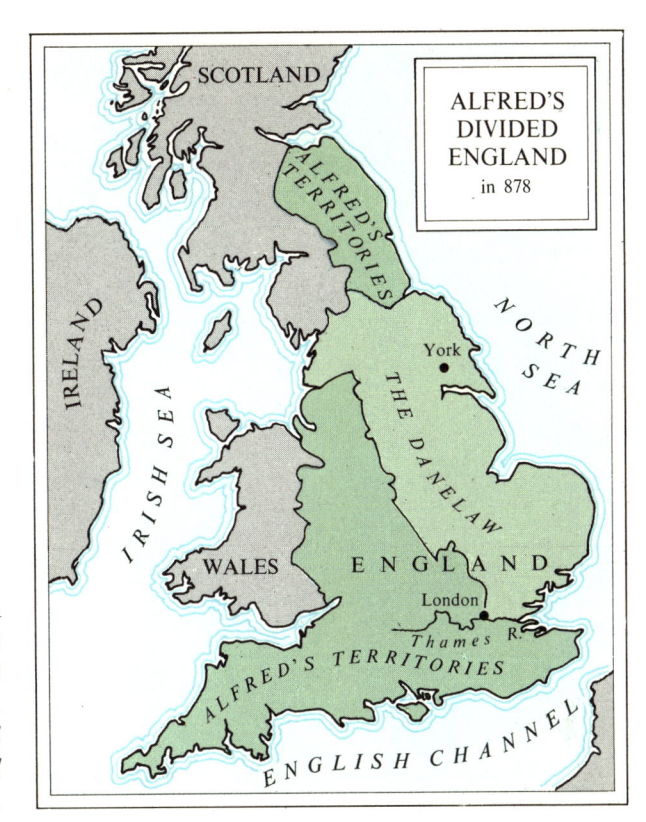

The map at right shows ninth-century England when it was divided into the kingdom under Alfred's rule and the Danelaw. The Roman name for York, capital of the Danelaw, was Eboracum—marked by the crown opposite the word "Ories" in the right margin of the thirteenth-century map at left. England was then no longer divided, but boundaries remained between England and Scotland (separated by two walls) and between England and Wales ("Walia").

TEXT CONTINUED FROM PAGE 47

Although Alfred's fleet was successful many times when it sailed forth to fight, his unskilled sailors often ran the vessels aground before they saw action. He had more success reorganizing the army. It had always been the practice to call out the forces for a particular campaign when danger threatened. When it was over the men went back to their farms. But Alfred divided the army into two parts with alternate duty; while one half went to battle, the other half tilled the land.

This gave him a standing army with which to meet the last great Viking threat of his reign. In 892 a fleet of 250 ships, fresh from an unsuccessful siege of Paris, landed an eight-thousand-man army on England's south coast. At the same time Hastings, the chief who had once raided into northern Italy, sailed up the Thames with another fleet of eighty vessels. These new invaders were joined by some discontented elements from the Danelaw, and it was three years before Alfred, in a series of brilliant maneuvers, finally defeated them. In the last clash he found the Northmen in a fortified camp on the Lea River twenty miles from London. Instead of attacking the camp, he obstructed the

By rotating his troops' terms of service, Alfred the Great was able to establish a fresh and willing army. Alfred's battlefield leadership was boldly imaginative, although he is not known to have employed any new formations or weapons. In the scene above, from a tenth-century psalter, a squad of English soldiers is being rallied by an angel armed with a bow and arrows and a sword; the soldiers carry long lances with tips similar to the contemporary point shown opposite. The manuscript drawing at right depicts how an English soldier dressed. Draped over a short, close-fitting tunic, his heavy cloak is fastened on the right shoulder with a brooch; below that he wears cross-gartered leggings and pointed shoes.

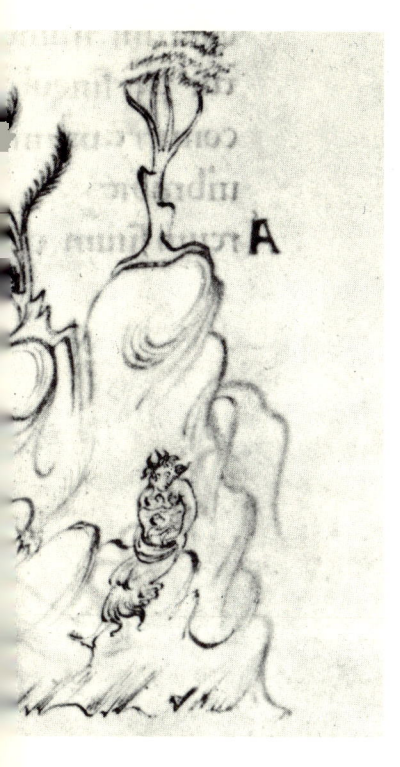

river channel below it. Deprived of the use of their ships, the Vikings abandoned their camp and struck across England on a forced march that took them to the Severn River. There they wintered and then dispersed, some to East Anglia, some to the Danelaw, some to seek land for themselves, and others to return to piracy on the Seine.

During the last decades of Alfred's life he found peace, quietly working on scholarly writings and translations. Among the works translated by the king and the learned clerics who assisted him is the *Seven Books of History Against the Pagans*, a voluminous survey written by the fifth-century priest Orosius. To his translation Alfred added several pages on a subject of great importance to himself and his people—the Northland. From Alfred's devotion to scholarship sprang the beginnings of English education. And to this legacy he added another important gift—a powerful and united kingdom. By defeating the Vikings in Wessex and by expanding his territory, Alfred had opened the way for his son Edward, who succeeded him in 899, to launch a decisive campaign against the Vikings who still remained in the Danelaw.

In Europe the pattern of Viking change was rather different. No task forces of Northmen appeared as they had in England, but raiding bands were larger than they had been in early ninth-century Europe and were more inclined to spend the winters on a coast where they found a good harbor. Also, traders from the Northland surged south, establishing depots where slaves and plunder might be stored and sold. Land-hungry farmers from Scandinavia and Denmark were looking for lands other than the Danelaw in which to resettle.

The Viking military groups of this time often seemed to be private armies led by chieftains to whom the men were pledged by ties of blood and feudal loyalty. And these Vikings had adopted fighting as a lifelong profession rather than a summer-time venture. Eventually one of these groups developed into the famous Jomsvikings, an order of Viking knights. In their strongholds (which probably resembled the large camps recently found on the Danish island of Zealand) they trained under a rigorous set of rules. No women were allowed in the fort, nor any man under eighteen or over fifty. Each Jomsviking took a vow that he would defend his companion like a brother. No man could utter a word of fear, no matter how hopeless things looked, and all plunder was deposited in a common pool to be equally divided. The Jomsviking Saga ends by saying, ". . .

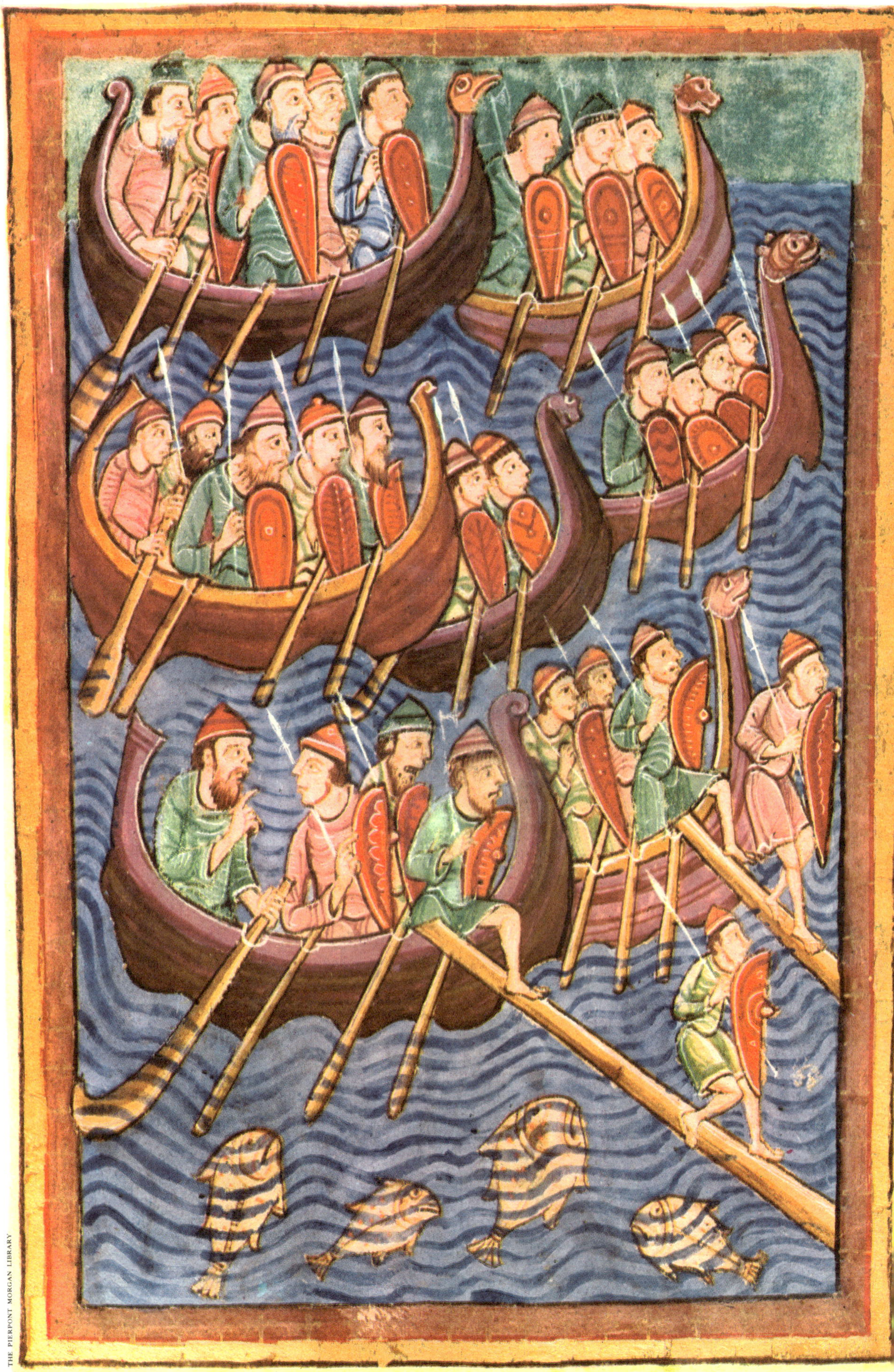

they went out and made war in different countries, got high renown, and were looked on as the greatest warriors."

Under the repeated blows of raids and invasion sorties, the old empire of Charlemagne continued to crumble and shrink. Frisia was almost entirely conquered and for a time became a Danish colony. Charles the Bald's kingdom of the Western Franks, with its many cities conveniently situated on rivers, suffered most heavily. Charles was a brave but not very competent ruler who believed, probably with good reason, that the Vikings were a minor menace compared to his own brothers and to the rebellious dukes of Aquitaine and Brittany. He preferred bribing the Northmen to go elsewhere rather than fighting them.

The greatest assault of the Viking Era took place in 885. Charles the Bald was dead by this time, and Charles the Fat ruled the West Frankish kingdom. But Charles was in Italy when the largest Viking fleet so far assembled appeared on the Seine late in November. If the chronicles can be believed, the force contained seven hundred large ships manned by forty thousand Northmen. The Vikings wanted to reach the rich territory of Burgundy; but Paris was between them and their objective. In those days most of Paris was on the island in the Seine where the Cathedral of Notre Dame now stands, but the island was walled and connected to both banks of the river by two bridges. While those bridges stood, the Vikings could not pass.

The Frankish chronicles say that the invaders were led by a Viking named Siegfried. He sought a parley with Jocelin, Bishop of Paris, and offered to spare the city if the Vikings might be allowed to pass upriver. Although he had but two hundred men in the city's garrison, Jocelin refused, and the Vikings attacked, aiming their thrust at an unfinished tower guarding the northern bridge.

The first day the Vikings assailed the tower with arrows and sling stones that merely stuck in or bounced off the tower's wooden walls. The arrows of the defenders found easy marks in the dense ranks of the attackers, and boiling oil and pitch sent singed and howling Vikings into the river to cool off. The Northmen withdrew at nightfall to burn their dead in their riverbank camp. In the ruddy

Danish Vikings, like those who went to England in the ninth century (left), later became less aggressive—in part because of improved English defenses, in part because of dissension at home. Denmark's King Harold Bluetooth was baptized (above), but his son rebelled and reverted to paganism.

glare of their pyres, the French labored through the night to complete their unfinished tower. The second day's attack was no more successful than the first, and the Vikings withdrew to dig in for what promised to be a long siege.

They also built several siege weapons: mangonels to heave large rocks, wheeled mantelets covered with skins to protect attackers as they approached the walls, and a unique multiple battering-ram that was described by a monk who witnessed the battle as "three machines of unequaled size, mounted on sixteen wheels, and fashioned of huge pieces of oak bound together. On each machine is placed a battering-ram, covered by a high roof. Within the house they could hold concealed, it is said, sixty men."

With these new weapons the Vikings again attacked in January and fought violently for three days. Flaming oil incinerated their battering-rams and the engineers inside. The Vikings fought fire with fire. When the wind was blowing upstream they fired three of their ships and set them sailing toward the wooden bridge, but the vessels burned out harmlessly against the stone piers. The attackers tried to fill the ditch around the tower with straw, branches, slaughtered animals, and the dead bodies of their prisoners. Nothing worked. The Parisians' banner still waved above the weary defenders, and at intervals the sacred bones of Saint Germain (a bishop of Paris) were taken from his crypt and carried around the ramparts—a ceremony that, according to the monk, caused the miraculous defeat of the pagans.

Again the Vikings retired and scoured the countryside for supplies for a long siege. In February, nature came to the help of the Northmen when a flood washed out the northern bridge, enabling part of the Viking fleet to pass upstream and harass the countryside to the Loire River. The remainder continued the siege, occasionally attacking the southern bridge.

And so passed the winter and the spring. Messengers from Paris had been sent to Charles the Fat with frantic appeals for help, and he was slowly making his way across the Alps. Siegfried finally tired of the siege and offered to leave if he received a payment of sixty pounds of silver. This was agreed to, but most of the Vikings refused to follow Siegfried when he left with his personal band.

The siege continued, and in August the Vikings began a full-scale attack on Paris. This time help was at hand for the Parisians. Charles the Fat made his appearance on the heights of Montmartre with a formidable army and drove

TEXT CONTINUED ON PAGE 60

This nineteenth-century reconstruction of a Viking attack on Paris is drawn looking upriver, to the east. The ancient towers and battlements are bristling with defenders who have succeeded in burning the Vikings' batteringrams, throwing down their assault ladders, and repulsing their attack.

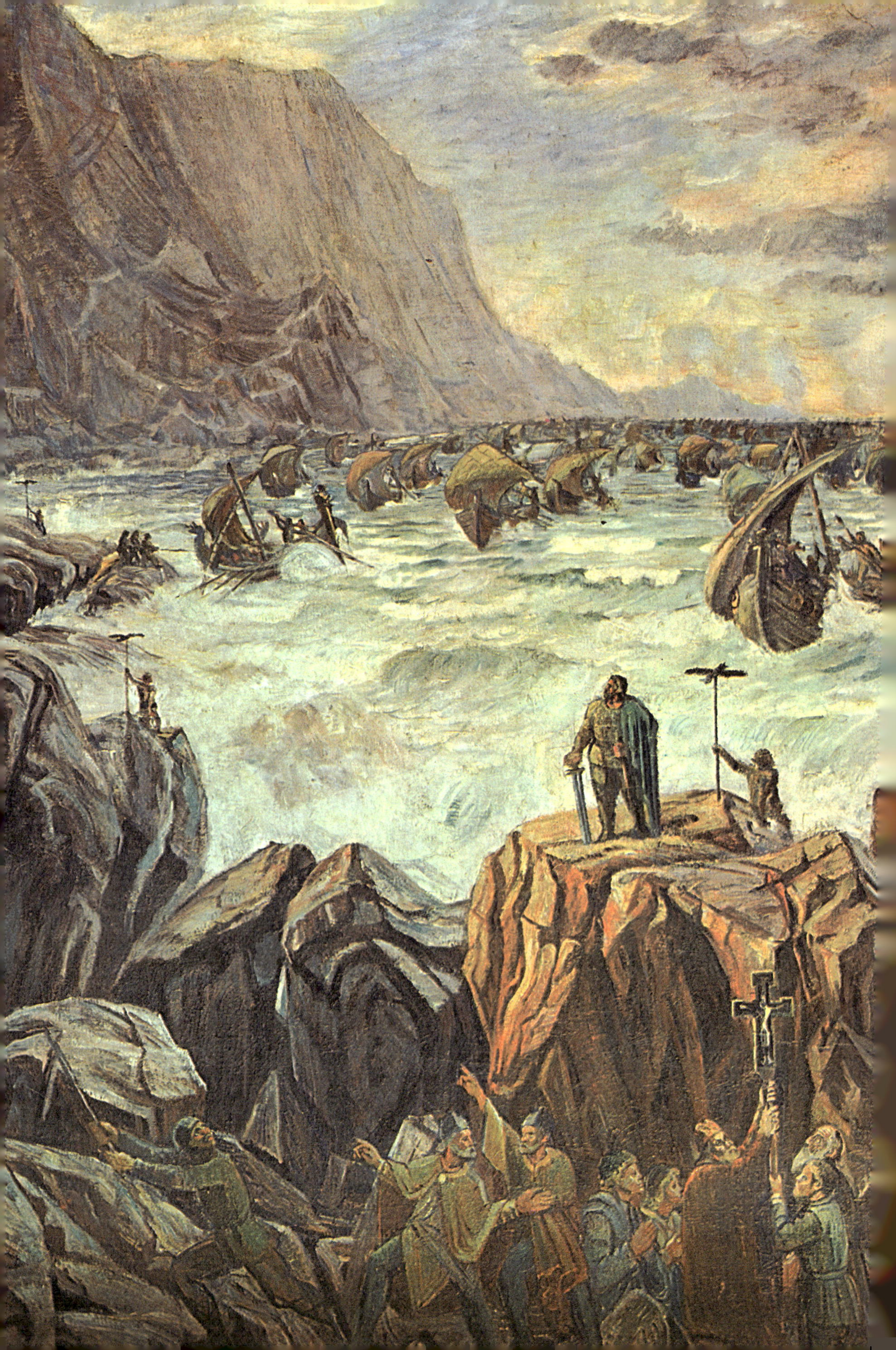

In 1911, over one thousand years after the event, a Danish artist painted this scene of Rollo's Viking fleet approaching the coast of Normandy. Yet many of the details of the painting seem accurate: the vast number of ships in the fleet, the design of the ships' steering oars, and the eagle standard being held up beside Rollo as he surveys the cliffs at the mouth of the Seine. In the foreground, Frankish defenders and monks prepare to flee.

59

TEXT CONTINUED FROM PAGE 56

the Vikings back to their camp across the Seine. The time was now ripe for a decisive battle against the enemy, but Charles backed down. Instead he made an agreement with the invaders that allowed them free passage up the Seine into Burgundy, where they could winter. Charles also offered to pay them seven hundred pounds of silver if they promised to leave his kingdom the following spring. The brave Parisians protested Charles' action and even banded together to try and prevent the Vikings from passing up the Seine—but to no avail. In the spring of 889, the Vikings returned to claim their seven hundred pounds of silver, and this time the Parisians fought, driving the invaders off once and for all. The Viking fleet never again visited the courageous city.

For almost twenty years the country was free of Vikings. Then, in 911, a new Viking leader made his appearance on the lower Seine. The French called him Rollo, the Northmen, Rolf. Not much is known about him—it is not even certain whether he was Danish or Norwegian. Although he was probably the latter, his band was mixed, with a majority of Danes. By this time Charles the Simple was king of the West Franks.

Charles was not as simple as his name implied. He knew that he could not dislodge Rollo from his fortified base on the lower Seine, and that paying continued tribute was a waste of money. He therefore offered to give the Vikings a province of their own—all the land between the lower Seine and the coast of what is now called Normandy —if Rollo would become a Christian, swear allegiance to Charles, and agree to help protect the heartland of Charles' kingdom from other Vikings. Rollo accepted the offer and became the first Duke of Normandy; the Vikings had a permanent home in the land now known as France.

Rollo enlarged his province, somewhat at the expense of neighboring Brittany, and settled down to become a Frenchman. He kept his promise to Charles and helped unite France by joining with the king to subdue the rebellious Duke of Burgundy. Rollo's son William Longsword continued this policy, and when Rollo's grandson Richard talked of returning to Viking paganism, his thoroughly Christianized knights would have no part of it. These were no longer pagan Northmen; they had become completely French in dress, manners, language, customs, and religion. They stood guard to protect their new homeland from their old countrymen; after Rollo, France was forever free from new territorial conquests by Northmen.

This statue of Rollo, the Viking Duke of Normandy, is in Rouen.

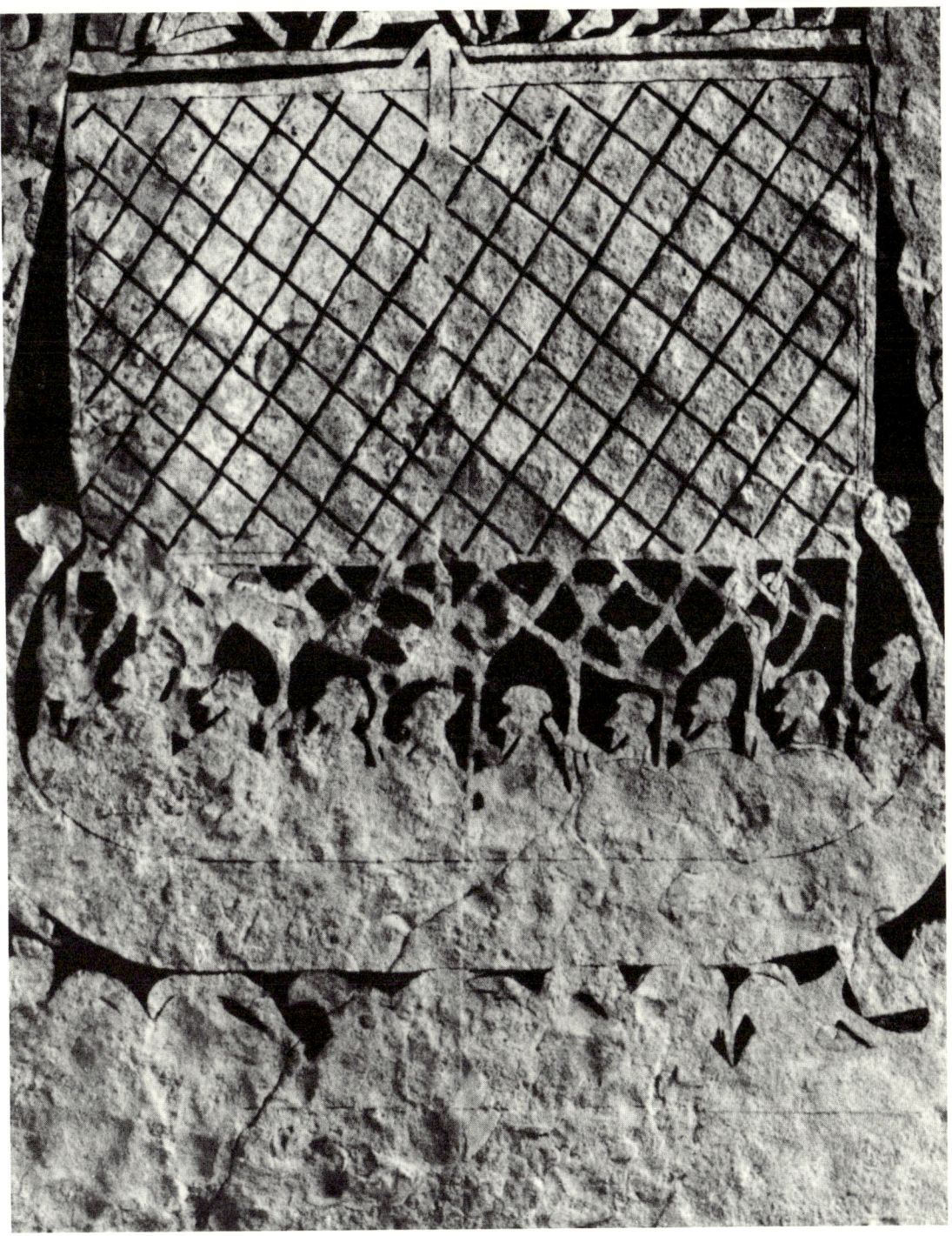

Vikings eager for plunder continued to arrive on the coast of Europe even after Rollo's acquisition of Normandy and throughout the first half of the tenth century. They sailed in double-ended vessels like this one carved on a Viking rune stone; some naval scholars believe that the intricate system of clue lines enabled the Northmen to reef, or shorten, the large sail.

IV VIKINGS OF THE EAST

62

In 859, not long before the men of the Great Army clambered aboard their dragon ships and sailed westward toward the invasion of England, a smaller Viking band prepared an expedition toward the east. Raising their billowing single sails on heavy yardarms, they moved out onto the gray, wind-swept waters of the Baltic Sea.

They followed a route taken by many Northmen before them, pressing on to the easternmost shore of the Gulf of Finland. That fertile coastal region was gradually being brought under the control of settlers from Sweden. But this band of Viking raiders was not interested in farming. Having heard of Novgorod, a prosperous inland trading town at the head of riverways that stretched south and east, they soon left the coast behind them. With their superior weapons and well-practiced tactics, they fell upon the city and seized it from its Slavic citizens. Then, according to one of the earliest Russian histories, the Northmen de-

Flags flying and pipes playing, two ships with overlapped shields close for combat in a scene from a tenth-century manuscript. The Vikings fought in river boats like these for control of Russia's waterways; one sailor has been cast overboard.

manded a large ransom, and having obtained it, returned to their homes in Sweden.

Not only was this the first eastward Viking raid to be recorded, but it was the beginning of another large-scale Viking expansion. For the easy capture of Novgorod came to the ears of an ambitious Swedish nobleman named Rurik; he decided to abandon his unsuccessful attempts to claim a territory for himself in Western Europe and turn his attention to the eastern shores of the Baltic Sea. Most of Rurik's career is known only through inexact and romantic writings, but he is generally regarded by historians as the founder of Russia's first royal house.

It appears that Rurik arrived on the Baltic coast of Russia around 860. He probably landed with a sizable number of troops, officers, and men who had fought under him bravely in Scandinavia and Europe. To the rough and turbulent Slavic tribes who lived in Russia then, the appearance of this new force—battle-ready and tightly disciplined—must have been overwhelmingly impressive. The earliest Russian description of these years, a long account known as the Ancient Chronicle, states that the primitive Slavs then asked the Vikings (whom they called Varangians) to come inland and rule their cities. One version of the chronicle claims that the Slavs called to the Vikings, "Our land is great and rich, but there is no order in it. Come to rule and reign over us!"

The story may be nothing more than a romantic cover up for Rurik's conquest of the territory surrounding Novgorod. But there may be some basis in fact for the story; some historians believe that the trade routes south to Constantinople had been blocked by hostile tribes and that the Slavs

TEXT CONTINUED ON PAGE 68

The three drawings above were made to illustrate the Ancient Chronicle, the earliest Russian story of that nation's origins. Among many other historical legends it tells how Rurik's lieutenants Askold and Dir took over Kiev (far left); how Rurik's descendant Yaroslav was enthroned as prince of Kiev (center); and how Vikings fought among themselves for Novgorod and Kiev (right). The map below shows these locations in Viking Russia.

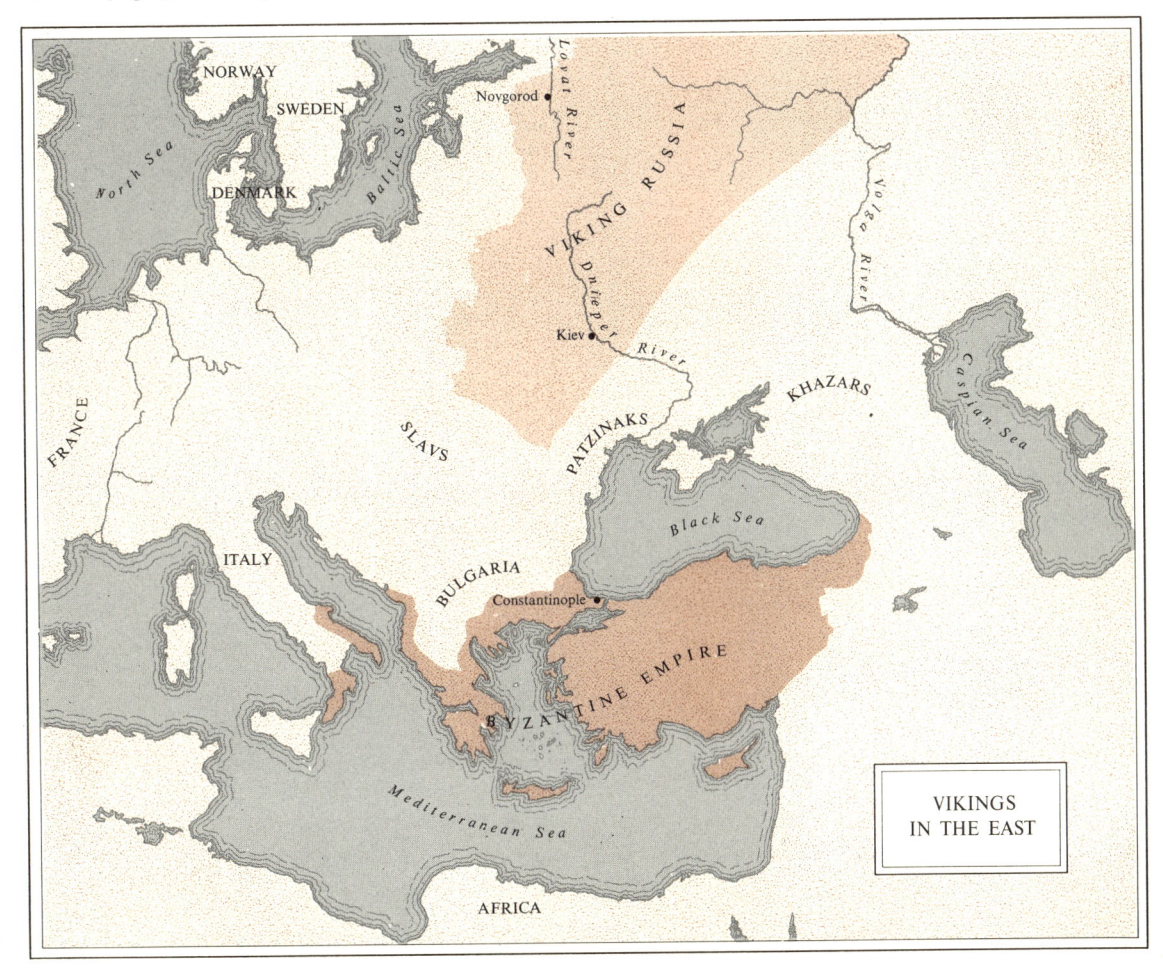

VIKINGS IN THE EAST

+LIGNO QUO CHRISTUS HUMANUM SUBDIDIT HOSTEM DAT ROMAE IUSTINUS OPEM ET SOCIA DECOREM

THE GOLDEN CITY

When the Vikings began to cruise down the waterways of Russia, Constantinople (present-day Istanbul) was both a treasure house of ancient riches and the flourishing center of the mighty Byzantine Empire. Much of the wealth of Rome had been taken there by the Emperor Constantine when he moved his capital from Rome in 330; the greatest artisans of the Christian world had been working ever since to produce magnificent church ornaments such as the jeweled, silver-gilt cross at left. Golden Constantinople beckoned the Vikings with irresistible force—to trade, to plunder, to fight. The city was highly accessible, located on the Bosporus strait and split by an inlet invitingly called the Golden Horn, which runs across the top of the old map of Constantinople at right. But it was stoutly defended. Although Byzantine noblemen such as those seen below at a feast seemed luxury-ridden and decadent to the Vikings, their troops could fight. These land and sea forces held off the Vikings; they also served as a bulwark against invasions of Europe by Eastern conquerors up to the mid fifteenth century when Constantinople's gold finally fell to the Turks.

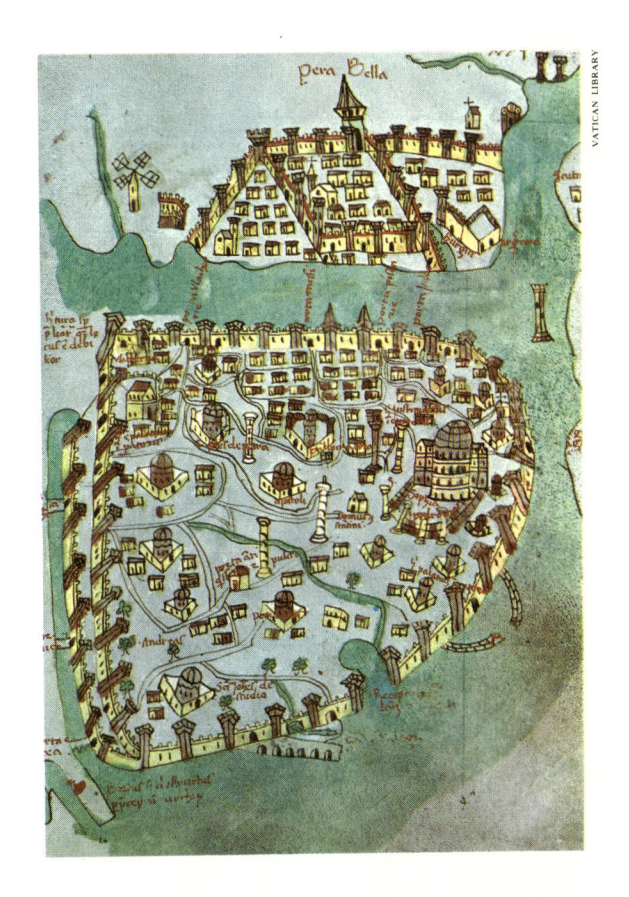

TEXT CONTINUED FROM PAGE 64

realized they needed a powerful military force to help them break through. Whatever the truth of "the Calling of the Varangians," as this episode is known, Rurik and his lieutenants now became as firmly entrenched in Novgorod as the descendants of Ivar the Boneless were in England's Danelaw.

One name used to categorize the Vikings who followed Rurik was Varangians; another was Rus, and it is from that word that *Russia* is derived. The origins of the word Rus cannot be traced with any certainty, but some scholars believe Rus merely means red or ruddy and refers to the appearance of the big, red-haired men who had come to reign over the Slavs—and to look for new lands to conquer. Other scholars believe the word is associated with the Finnish word *ruotsi*, which means "rowing folk" or "river folk." And to the Vikings living in Novgorod, Russia was indeed a country of wide, navigable rivers—stretching like highways toward such brilliant centers of trade and culture as Baghdad in Persia, and Constantinople, capital of the Byzantine Empire.

At first the Russian Vikings were content to trade with their neighbors in furs, wax, honey, and slaves. Then they found it convenient to set up new trading centers and to seize others, like the important trading village of Kiev. After that they recognized that by piracy and terror they could strip the countryside of its wealth faster and more easily than by trade. They demanded tribute from tribes living on the rivers, and in their swift, red-painted ships they rowed and sailed farther and farther south.

Inevitably, some of the bolder Vikings pushed all the way down the Dnieper and reached the Black Sea. Two of Rurik's lieutenants, Askold and Dir, led the first Viking attack on the Byzantine capital. With loot as their object, they sailed along the western shore of the Black Sea and appeared under the walls of Constantinople with a fleet of two hundred boats.

They had picked their time well. The Emperor Michael III was away with the fleet fighting Saracens. The home garrison could have withstood a Viking raid on the high-walled city, but according to the romantic Ancient Chronicle, Constantinople had no need to protect itself by fighting. The bishop of the city merely took the robe of the Virgin Mary from its sacred shrine in the Blachernae Chapel and dipped it in the waters of the Bosporus. Immediately "a storm of wind came up, and when great waves straightway rose, confusing the boats of the godless Rus, it threw them upon the shore and broke them up, so that few escaped such destruction and returned to their native land."

While the Viking leaders Askold and Dir were pioneering in the south, Rurik continued to extend the territory of the Rus in the north. When he died in 879, he was succeeded by Oleg, another Viking chieftain who reigned as regent for Rurik's infant son. Oleg, who seems to have been unwilling to tolerate any rivals, soon paid a visit to Kiev. The town was too strong to attack, so Oleg lured its rulers, Askold and Dir, onto his ship and slew them. He then moved his capital to Kiev and set himself up as its prince, ruling wisely and well until the year 912. Thus, Oleg, rather than Rurik, is considered the first Russian crowned head. He brought the eastern Slavs under his control and built up a mighty confederacy of town-provinces ruled by Viking princes. He fortified the borders of his empire against the fierce Khazars to the east, around the mouth of the Volga River, and the savage Patzinaks, who ruled the Dnieper River delta. His horsemen and his fleet guarded the long river-route to the riches of the East.

A bearded monk named Nestor (above) wrote parts of the poetical Ancient Chronicle; he worked in the Pechersky Monastery in Kiev at the end of the eleventh century. More of a patriot than a scholar, he wove into history the tale that Rurik's Vikings had been "called" to rule Russia. Yet Nestor also included many inglorious events (Igor's defeat at Constantinople) and strange fancies (Olga's hideous revenge against the Drevlianians).

λοχωϊποιεςαυτοις · Καιπολλφιζίωκαταπλεξαμψοι · πολλαμβρωνπαδροιοέχου
πυρρικῶν · Αραδὲκαιπῶσκαδιπυρπολοῦπυρί

τολεπωπω̑ πυρπολ τοντωνὲναντίφλον

Ηλικωνπαρλωξέωκνομέρωντονπαθοισι · Καιπροςτονκαιστοςβλαχρῶνκαταραιεσε

οιρωμαιοιδιώκον   οιρωςφεντν

Constantinople continued to tempt the Russian Vikings. Its treasure seemed the ultimate prize for their adventurous spirits and powerful swords. Both as the great trading center of the eastern Mediterranean and as the capital of Eastern Christendom, it was fabulously wealthy. Its churches and shrines contained fortunes in gold and gems. The Vikings gathered their forces to make a second massive assault.

According to the Ancient Chronicle, Oleg stormed southward to Constantinople in 907 with eighty thousand men in two thousand ships and in cavalry detachments that moved along the riverbank parallel to the fleet. The Byzantine Greeks of Constantinople had shut up their walled city, but Oleg found a way to reach the suburbs and plunder them. A chain had been stretched across the harbor (the Golden Horn) to keep the Vikings out, so Oleg hauled his ships onto land, put wheels under some of them, and proceeded cross-country. At this point the Byzantine emperor realized the determination of the Vikings; finally, during a truce, he offered tribute and a very favorable trade agreement.

This trade agreement between the Vikings and the Byzantines stipulated that the Northmen could enter Constantinople through one gate only, in small groups and unarmed. But bolder Vikings dreamed of being let loose within the city to pillage and plunder. When Oleg was succeeded by Igor, that Viking leader could not resist trying his luck assaulting the Byzantine capital. He sailed down the Dnieper with a fleet variously reported to have one thousand to ten thousand vessels. When Igor reached Constantinople, all the Byzantine fleet, except for fifteen leaky vessels, was again away chasing Saracens in the Mediterranean Sea. A brave Byzantine admiral armed each of these old barks with a machine for throwing Greek fire and sailed out to protect the Bosporus. A blazing death poured from the machines on the Byzantine vessels into the open boats of the Vikings. Overwhelmed, they retired from before the city and turned to plundering the countryside. The Ancient Chronicle says that "many sacred churches they gave to the flames, while they burned many monasteries and villages and took no little booty on both sides

Byzantine cavalrymen pursue three Russian Vikings in the scene at left from the famous eleventh-century manuscript by John Skylitzes. Above it, Byzantine sailors pour Greek fire from a bow nozzle into an opponent's boat.

of the sea. Of the people they captured, some they butchered, some they set up as targets and shot at, some they seized upon, and after tying their hands behind their backs, they drove nails through their heads."

While the Vikings were engaged in these gruesome practices the Greeks collected an army, and when their great fleet of majestic triremes returned from the Mediterranean, they defeated Igor decisively on land and sea. Igor escaped with a handful of men and soon raised a greater army to return to the attack. This time, before they even reached the Bosporus, they were met by gift-bearing Greeks who came as emissaries of the emperor, and the commercial treaty was renewed.

On the way back to Kiev, Igor imprudently stopped off with a small detachment to exact additional tribute from the Drevlianians. This Slavic tribe, apparently feeling that they were already paying enough, killed the Viking prince. His widow, Olga, was a fierce woman, and her revenge was long and dreadful. As a result of her vengeance, the Drevlianian tribe was virtually annihilated. Having accomplished that, Olga settled down to a wise and profitable reign, which included a peaceful trip to Constantinople where she was entertained in splendor by the Byzantine emperor and became a Christian. Her son Svyatoslav would have none of this new faith, and he became a cross between a Viking and a Cossack.

A vivid portrait of Svyatoslav exists that shows him as more of a Slav than a Northman. It was left by a contemporary Byzantine historian who wrote that Svyatoslav ". . . came across the river in a Scythian [Russian] boat, rowing with his men. He was of medium height, broad-shouldered, with a long and luxurious mustache. His nose was stubby, eyes blue and eyebrows bushy, and his head was shaven, apart from a lock on one side, which was a sign of nobility. In one ear was a gold ring with two pearls and a ruby between them; his white gown differed from his men's only by being cleaner; he appeared brooding and wild." This was distinctly a man of the North, a descendant of Rurik, but it was becoming harder to tell him apart from the Slavic peoples he ruled. The Vikings were becoming Russians.

There were, however, Vikings who remained distinctly Vikings and seemed unable or disinclined to lose their distinctive identity in the destiny of any one nation. Such a Viking was Harold Hardrada, who came to Russia as one of many refugee noblemen from war-ravaged eleventh-

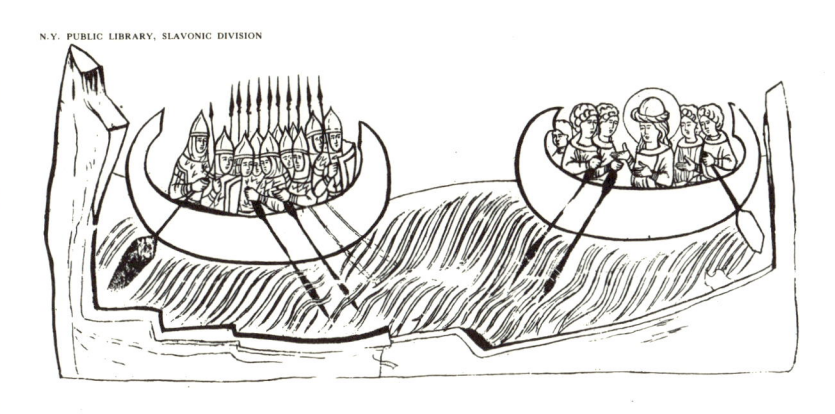

The Viking ships that sailed in Igor's armada against Constantinople probably resembled the deep-drafted, double-ended river boats in the drawing at left. The ships of the Byzantine navy had one or two banks of oars, curved sternposts, and two pipes at the bow for discharging Greek fire. Vessels of this description are shown in the contemporary battle scene below.

73

century Norway. Harold arrived in Kiev at the age of fifteen, fresh from the battlefield on which his half-brother King Olaf II was slain while defending his Norwegian throne. From Kiev, which by then had become a substantial city and one in which Harold rapidly found employment as an officer with the palace troops, he sailed down the Dnieper to become the leader of the Varangian Guard in Constantinople.

The Byzantine emperors had a passion for tall, strong warriors in their personal guard, and Vikings became the royal troops of the palace, the Varangian Guard whom the Byzantines called axe-bearing barbarians. The value of this guard to the emperor lay not only in the skill and valor of Vikings as warriors but in their incorruptible loyalty when they had taken an oath of allegiance and in their contempt for the palace jealousies and intrigues. They were well paid and had ample opportunity for plunder, particularly when led by Harold Hardrada, an outstanding strategist and apparently something of a diplomat. He wangled a fortune from the emperor, married a Russian princess, and finally took half of Norway from his nephew.

Not long after Harold had taken over the command of the Varangian Guard, it was ordered out on an extensive campaign that eventually took him as far south as the Euphrates River in Persia. Legends credit him with capturing eighty Arab cities, the loot from which he sent back to Constantinople. Later he turned back to threaten Jerusalem, then under Arab control. While he was preparing to attack the Holy City the caliph made a treaty with the emperor guaranteeing Christians access to its shrines, and Harold was recalled to Constantinople. He next led the Varangian Guard to Sicily where he captured four strong walled cities by different ruses. On one of these occasions he tunneled from a sunken riverbed under the walls of a castle to come up inside the dining hall at mealtime. In another instance he surrounded a city but made no effort to attack. Instead, he had some of his men play games just out of arrow range of the walls. After a few days of this, the defenders, curious as to the strange games, came outside the gate to watch. The Vikings edged nearer and nearer in their play until they were close enough to whip their swords from under their cloaks and make a dash

On a white horse, Svyatoslav appears twice in this ancient Bulgarian drawing. Both times he looks more like a Russian knight than a Viking chieftain.

рꙋскыи плѣкъ на блъгары

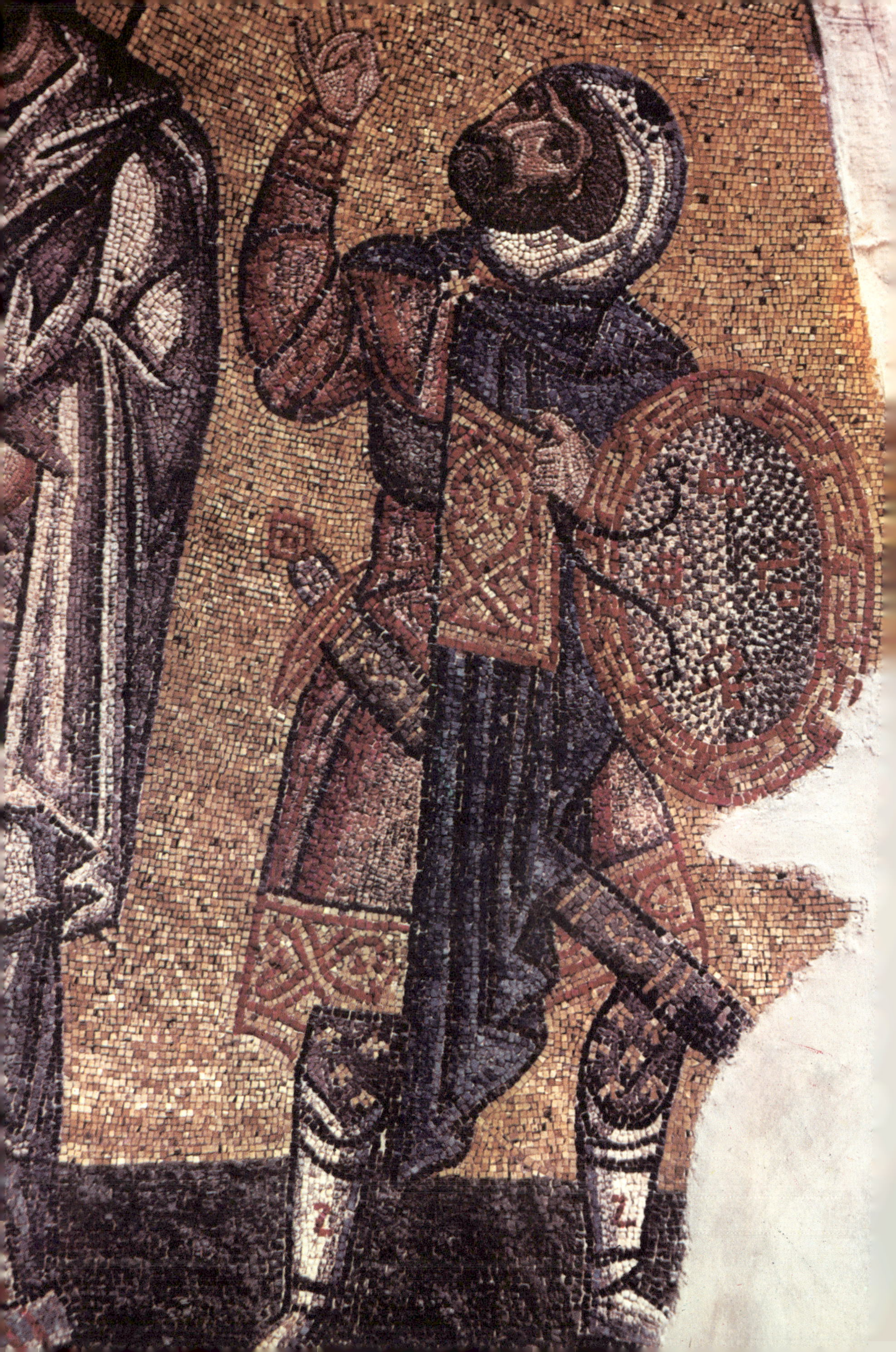

for the gate, holding it until the main body came out of hiding.

When Harold returned to Constantinople, he was a wealthy man from his share of the Near Eastern and Sicilian loot. He enhanced his wealth by participating several times in an unusual ceremony, held on state occasions, in which the officers of the Varangian Guard were allowed to walk through the emperor's treasure chamber and take all that they could carry away. Seven-foot Harold could carry quite a load. This, with his other loot, he sent back to Kiev for safekeeping. That pleasant condition continued until the emperor died and an upstart of another dynasty came to the throne. The new ruler, Michael V, alienated Harold by persecuting the Empress Zoë, widow of Harold's former employer. When the city revolted and the mob cornered the new emperor and his hated minister in a church, Harold made no effort to lead the Varangian Guard to their rescue. In fact, when the mob dragged its victims out, Harold personally gouged out their eyes.

Harold stayed in the east for about eight years. Then, in 1042, he learned that his nephew, Magnus the Good, had attained the throne of Norway. Harold felt that he had as much right to the throne as Magnus. He left Constantinople, stopped in Kiev long enough to pick up his wealth and a bride—a granddaughter of Svyatoslav's—and then proceeded to Sweden, where his wife's cousin was king and where he hoped to gather forces to fight Magnus.

Magnus the Good was a reasonable man. He might beat Harold and a Swedish army in battle. But Harold was famed as the greatest of generals—he was also the richest Viking. Therefore Magnus proposed a peaceful meeting at which it was finally agreed that if Harold would give Magnus half his wealth, Magnus would give Harold half his kingdom. The alliance proved unexpectedly rewarding for Harold, particularly when Magnus died two years later and left Harold undisputed king.

Harold Hardrada had been a leading Viking in the eastward Viking adventures. Then in the North he ruled for nineteen years as king of Norway. Later he would turn his eyes westward and lead the last great Viking invasion of England in 1066.

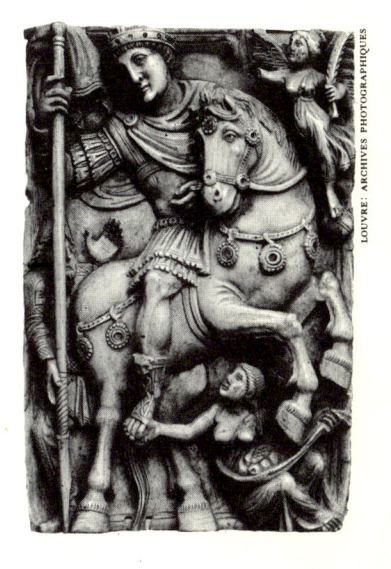

Byzantine rulers—like the emperor above, carved in ivory—had a need for large and loyal defenders. The Vikings who took this service dressed in the style of the hooded guardsman in the eleventh-century mosaic at left.

V

BURIED PLUNDER

Archaeologists are learning more about the Vikings every year by burrowing in the earth to disclose relics of the long-dead past. Some of their finds confirm the stories in the sagas and chronicles, as in the case of the battle-axes found in the Thames River at the site of the old London Bridge. But other finds upset previous ideas and point to new theories about the Vikings. One of the most intriguing glimpses into the Viking Era is possible through the treasure hoards that have come to light. These consist principally of silver in bulk, silver ornaments (fragments of looted brooches and religious objects), and coins—there is relatively little gold. The hoards are seldom found in graves; they are simply buried treasure. And most of them are found by chance rather than by science—one was uncovered by a dog burying a bone. The amount of silver that has been unearthed indicates not only the Vikings' love for this precious metal but the success of their raiding and trading; there were no known native sources of silver in the Northland at the time. In one small area, the island of Gotland off the southeast coast of Sweden, the earth has given up more than 110,000 coins, over 1,000 ornaments, and 2,300 pieces of silver in bars, rings, or rods. A single hoard that was found in Russia weighed over two hundred pounds.

Scientists believe that the known hoards represent but a small fraction of the treasure that was originally hidden in the earth. Many finds have not been recorded—farmers who have inadvertently plowed up treasure pieces have seldom been scrupulous enough to report them. And other hoards buried deep in the ground may never be found.

A carved bow (above) was one of the first discovered parts of the famous Oseberg ship, which was rebuilt and moved to a Norwegian museum (right). Many current ideas about Viking customs and beliefs are based on this find.

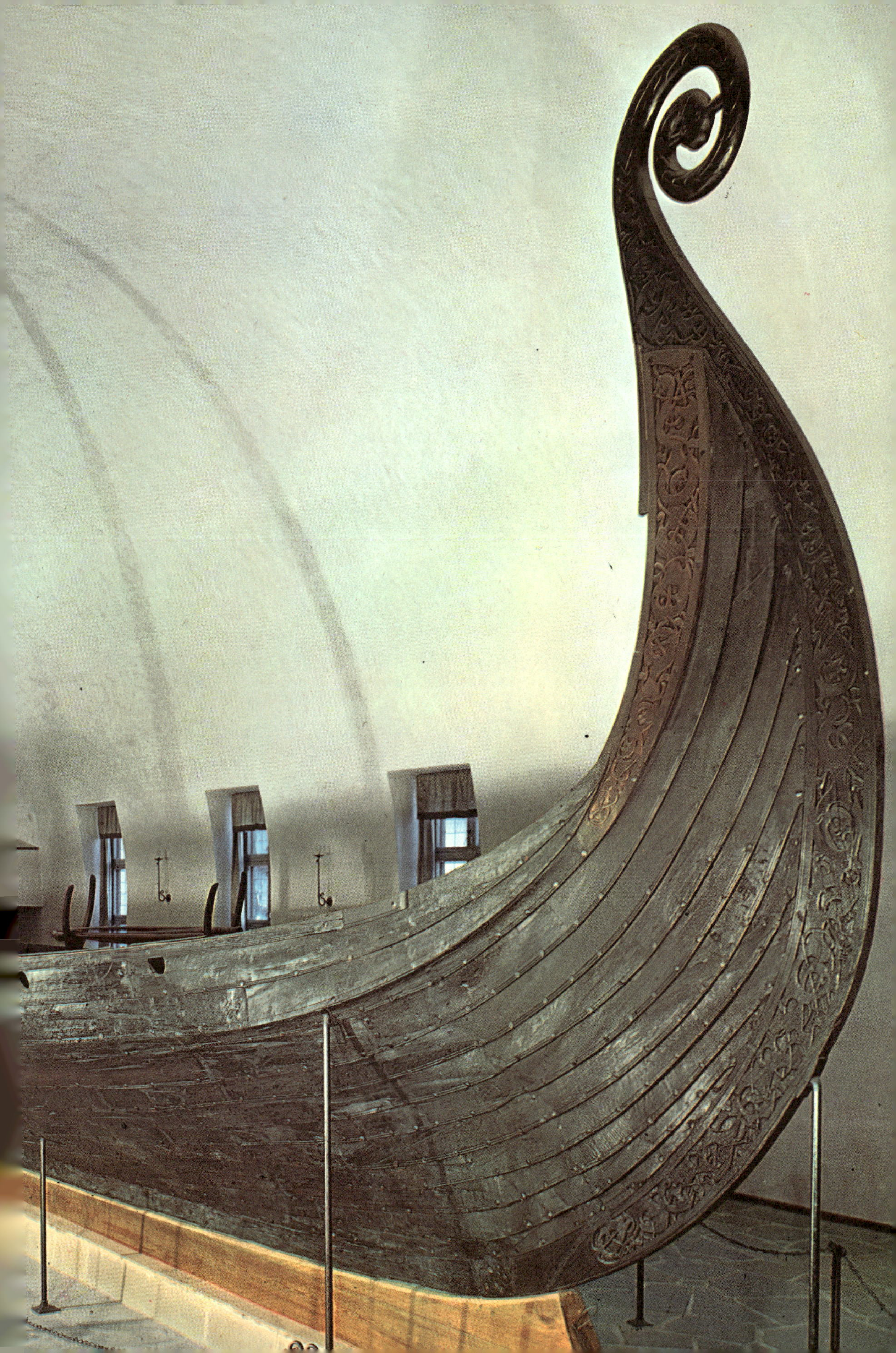

Horses have been found in several Viking graves. A bridle for one of these animals is pictured below; it is lavishly crafted and resembles the one worn by the horse opposite. Another object made for a Viking cavalryman is the harness ornament above, which is shaped like a mask.

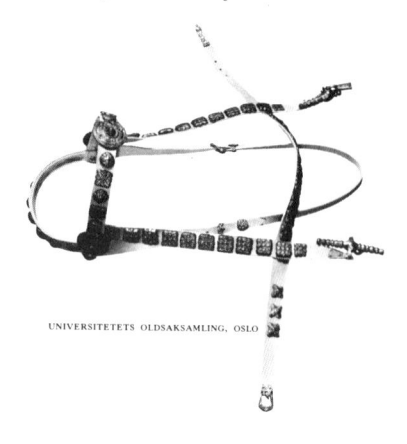

The ornaments and coins in the hoards are particularly valuable to modern researchers because of the information they provide on where the Vikings went and when. The coins, which are mostly Arabic, bear dates and figures that can still be read. They support other evidence that the Swedish Vikings reached the rich centers of Eastern trade via the rivers of Russia and the Black Sea; there they exchanged their slaves and plunder for glittering cash. And the ornaments indicate that the wealth won by the Vikings in raids on Europe was in the form of merchandise, portable valuables, and bulk silver.

As archaeology has become more scientific during the last century—particularly during the last few decades—all of its discoveries produce a more vivid, exact picture of the historic Viking. The emerging picture now shows that a typical Viking warrior dressed in a short coat of chain mail worn over a long woolen shirt gathered at the waist by a leather belt. Over that was a cloak of wool or animal skin clasped with an elaborately carved brooch. Unless he was an important chieftain, his head was probably protected by a simple metal hat with nose and cheek guards rather than by a fancy horned or crested helmet. He may have carried a thrusting spear about eleven feet long or several light throwing spears. His sword was slung over his shoulder and hung down his back. He had an axe and probably a short, single-edged knife thrust through his belt. In his left hand he carried a round shield. Assuming that he was not armed, he probably wore carved arm bands of silver and perhaps bracelets, for Vikings were inordinately fond of jewelry.

Thousands of graves have yielded examples of Viking weapons and equipment. Viking warriors are usually shown with swords or axes, and the sagas most frequently mention these potent weapons. Grave finds also indicate that spears were plentiful. These were of several types: heavy spears for thrusting, short, light ones for throwing, simple iron pikes, and a kind of halberd—a combined axe and spear with a long handle. Types of spearheads that have been found also vary widely. Some are very long and slim, others short and blunt. Some are shaped like arrowheads, some like harpoons, and some like fish spears with teeth pointing backward to inflict horrible wounds when they were pulled out.

The sword was obviously the Vikings' most prized weapon, though surely not the most common. The best-known type of Viking sword had a broad, double-edged

A colorful detail from a twelfth-century tapestry shows a Northman on a piebald horse. The knight has a pointed shield and wears a long mail shirt.

blade, but the narrow-bladed, single-edged *scramasax* (of Frankish origin) was sometimes carried instead. Both had straight blades. Most swords were ornamented, ranging from simple hilts and pommels of carved iron to rich handles and scabbards inlaid with precious metals. One short, double-edged sword found in southern Russia had a scabbard of solid gold.

Often imported to the Northland from workshops on the Rhine, most of the sword blades were laminated and damascened—made from several layers or rods fused together and twisted, then sliced to give a wavy, serpentine pattern to the blade. A surprising knowledge of the characteristics of metal is indicated by some swords that were made from alternate layers of iron and carbon-free steel, which would provide a blade better suited to the cold northern climate than the all-steel weapons of the south. Skilled as smiths and metalworkers, the Vikings could rival most of the swordmakers of Europe and the Near East. Most Viking swords had an indented ridge running the length of the blade which the sagas call the blood channel. According to the sagas some swords were heirlooms handed down from father to son; the Vikings gave these weapons fanciful names such as Gleam of Battle, Serpent of

Around the rim of the helmet above march little Viking warriors, the helmet maker, an early Viking craftsman, depicted heroes not as lordly individuals but as small figures in strange settings. But Viking craftsmen were intrigued by animals, especially such fanciful ones as the monster at right.

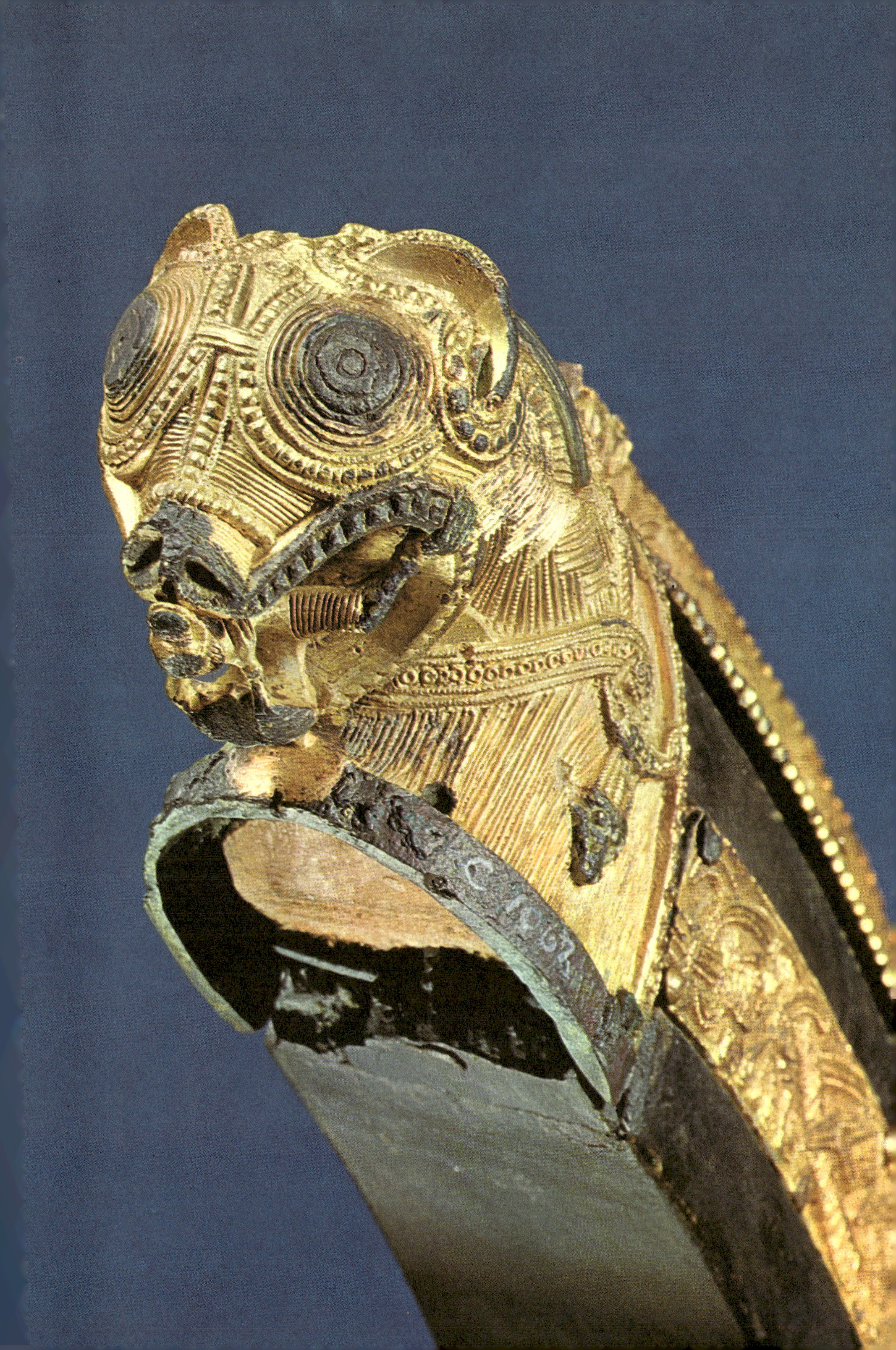

ARMS AND THE MAN

Archaeology and myth agree that the Viking fighting man was well-built, stalwart, and proud of his appearance. As well as carrying a sharply tipped spear and a circular wooden shield, the Viking in this sketch has a battle-axe at his belt and a strap over his shoulder to hold a yard-long sword (like the one at right below). His mail tunic resembles the relic below, and his trousers are bound with cross-garters. A conical helmet (also seen in the carving at far right) and a splendid cloak complete the dress of this sumptuously accoutered warrior.

84

the Wound, Fire of the Sea Kings, Thorn of the Shields.

Axes are the weapons most commonly associated with the Vikings, and axeheads found in Viking graves are of many types. They range from those with broad, curved cutting edges, like the traditional executioner's axe, to axes that resemble Indian tomahawks. The former type are obviously battle-axes, but most of the axes found were probably tools rather than weapons, or a combination of both. Some axeheads are richly engraved, indicating that axes, like swords, were highly prized possessions.

The basic armor of the Viking was the *brynja*, a flexible shirt made from linked iron rings. No plate armor has been found, although there are references to it in the sagas. Most of the few helmets that have been found are simple metal hats, some with nose guards. Carvings on metal ornaments and stones show Vikings with horned helmets and helmets decorated with bear and wolf heads, but these seem to have been the rare headgear of kings or chieftains.

The sagas also tell of men being carried on their shields and also taking shelter under them, and some rock carvings depict long, pointed shields covering most of the body. But no shields of this type have been found. The remains of shields that have been unearthed show that the shields were round, about three feet in diameter. They were made of wood, occasionally covered with leather, and painted. In some cases there was a rim of decorated metal around the edge. On the back there was a metal handle, and on the center of the front a raised metal knob of bronze or iron.

Mighty warrior or simple farmer, the Northman received a decent burial—and sometimes a magnificent one. Burial customs were extremely varied, and in examining the simple coffins, large burial chambers, and elaborate funerary ships in which the Vikings were interred, modern scholars have been able to find out much about their entire culture. The graves usually contained belongings of the deceased, and the wealthier or more prominent the person, the more lavish the burial.

Most lavish were the burials in ship graves, an honor that seems to have been reserved for royalty or noblemen. Stocked with household necessities as well as a rich variety of personal finery and ornaments, the vessels used for this purpose were also equipped with quantities of seamen's gear, as if the mourners actually expected that a long voyage would be undertaken. But so much mystery surrounds the ships—why are some moored to the land and others equipped with stowed anchors?—that it is difficult to get a clear idea of the Vikings' beliefs about the afterlife.

Some of the funeral ships were used not for burial but as pyres on which the noblemen were to be cremated. One of the most famous accounts of a Viking cremation was written by Ibn Fadlar, an Arab traveler who witnessed this pagan custom in Russia in the tenth century. After the body of a great chieftain had been set ablaze on a ship that was laden with jugs of liquor and food and even a slave girl, a Viking commented to the traveler: "You Arabs are foolish to put those you love and honor into the ground for earth and beasts and fields to eat them up: we burn them quickly, so they fly to paradise in an instant."

Much less impressive were the burial provisions for footsoldiers and farmers. In these simple graves, excavators have found tools and weapons and a few objects of some personal value. But there is no indication whether these were buried with the man because he was expected to use them in the afterlife, or if they were associated with some other religious belief (such as defense against evil spirits), or if they were simply buried with him because they were his.

Above ground there are other records of the Vikings on

carved stones which portray people or animals or scenes of Viking life. Scholars are not sure whether these pictures are symbolic or tell actual stories—about warriors falling off horses and sailors reaching port. Whatever their original purpose, the stones now yield information on such matters as ships' rigging and the number of oarsmen. Many of the stones also carry a message in an ancient alphabet of sixteen characters which the Northmen used to carve cryptic comments on ornaments and weapons as well. This alphabet, called the runic, was widely used in England and other Northern countries before being replaced by the Roman alphabet, and the stones on which these inscriptions are carved are called rune stones. Few of the myriad rune stones that have been found scattered throughout Scandinavia and the countries of Northern Euorope cast much light on the causes of the Viking expansion. But they do disclose many facts about Viking kings, warriors, and chieftains, and on occasion facts about Viking life itself. A rare type of inscription concerning the peaceful occupation of bridgebuilding read: "Holmfast had the ground cleared and a bridge built in memory of his father, Gier, who lived in Nasby." Other rune stones relate such

Much has been learned about Viking costumes from a tattered tapestry (left) in the Oseberg burial ship. Above, in a reconstructed section of eight-inch-wide tapestry, the first figure is a chief wearing a tightly fitted tunic and baggy trousers. Other significant figures, who appear to be leading an army of heavy battle-wagons, wear elaborate cloaks with pointed ends.

Although no Viking buildings have been found intact, some have been rebuilt based on still visible foundations. The pattern of postholes for a barracks in Denmark showed that the original building had long, curving sides; the reconstruction above followed that plan.

historical information as "Ale raised this stone in memory of himself. He received Cnut's geld in England. God bless his soul." The unknown and prideful Ale was also obviously a Christian, and the stone was erected after the year 1018 when the Danish King Cnut—or Canute—paid his army a bounty of geld and sent it home after he conquered England.

Other historical stones confirm the basic accuracy of some sagas, as in the case of Ingvar Vittefarne, a Swede who went *i viking* down the Volga River to the Caspian Sea, fighting dragons, serpents, and monsters on the way—according to the saga. The rune stone says nothing about these fearsome beasts, but it does place Ingvar and his brother at the mouth of the Volga River with the inscription "Yola set up this stone for his son Harold, Ingvar's brother; in far-off lands they sought wealth boldly; in the East their battles spread food before the eagle . . . in Sarkland [Eastern lands] they died."

A unique runic inscription is on the flanks of a twelve-foot marble lion in Venice. This is a Greek statue that was carved in the second or third century and brought to Venice from the harbor of Athens in the seventeenth century. On both flanks of the lion, Vikings had carved runic inscriptions that are now illegible. These Northmen may have been members of the Varangian Guard who fought in Greece, although there is no historical record that the Vikings ever reached Athens.

The most dramatic and informative finds of the archaeologists are several ships that had been drawn up on land and used as burial chambers. Two of these, the Gokstad ship found in 1880 and the Oseberg ship found in 1904, were almost perfectly preserved because they were buried in clay covered with peat and mounded over with dirt. What was unusual about the Oseberg ship was that it contained the skeletons of two women. It was rare to honor a woman with such an elaborate burial, and one theory is that the skeleton of the younger woman, who was about twenty-five or thirty when she died, was that of Queen Asa of Norway, who was known to have lived in the middle of the ninth century, the time that the find is dated. The other skeleton was that of a woman about sixty or seventy; possibly one of the queen's bondwomen sacrificed herself in order to serve her mistress in the afterworld. There are some isolated references in contemporary writings to sacrificing slaves and burying them with their masters, but it does not seem to have been a common practice.

The bodies of both women had been laid in a burial chamber, built aft of the mast, which was furnished with all the necessities of a bedroom, including rolled-up tapestries. Chests in the chamber contained household articles: iron scissors, lamps, looms, sewing boxes. In the stern of the ship were all kinds of kitchen utensils. In the bow were three beds, three sleighs, a beautifully decorated four-wheeled cart, two tents, a framework for a small house, and other useful items. In and around the ship were found the bones of at least ten horses, three dogs, and several oxen.

Historians take particularly great interest in the elaborate wood carving on the ship, cart, and sleighs. The work shows an advanced degree of skill in decorative carving, and some of the ornamentation tells much about the beliefs of the early Northmen. Fierce, grimacing animal heads were carved on the ends of several posts, and it is believed that these were meant to ward off evil spirits from the structures in which the posts were used.

The bow and the stern of the ship were carried up into

On the chest, back, and sides of this twelve-foot marble lion are runic inscriptions relating to the Vikings who served in the guard of the Byzantine emperor. Because the lion stood near Athens before being taken to Venice, it indicates Vikings may have reached Greece.

great, sweeping, richly carved curves ending with the head of a dragon, or serpent, topping both bow and stern. These heads were common on Viking ships both as decoration and for protection against evil spirits. One pagan belief was that the head should be removed before the ship made land so that it would not frighten the good spirits on shore. The heads, with their large glaring eyes, have caused the Viking vessels to be called dragon ships, but there is no evidence that the Northmen shared European or Oriental ideas of what dragons look like—with scales and wings and flashing eyes. The Vikings, however, did have definite ideas about sea serpents, and the carved heads and high pointed sterns of their ships were probably meant to represent serpents rather than conventional dragons.

The other important burial vessel is the Gokstad ship, which is dated around the year 900. Apparently it was an old vessel when it was buried, and it is believed that the skeleton found in it may be that of a chieftain who died about the end of the ninth century. Evidence that the chieftain had probably been *i viking* in Western Europe is provided by the skeleton of a peacock that was buried with him. The peacock was not native to Norway but was very

This view of the seventy-one-foot Oseberg ship shows her in 1904, shortly after the mound in which she was buried began to be excavated. The blue clay of the mound had kept her oak timbers in good condition, but centuries earlier, thieves had broken into the burial chamber (which has been removed in this photograph from the after part of the deck, background). Much jewelry had been taken, yet many fascinating and valuable items remained. Among them were kitchen utensils and various textiles; there were also several sleds like the one shown above and an intricately carved cart (top).

91

Valkyries were heavenly maidens who the Vikings believed carried slain warriors from the battlefield to Valhalla. In this group of carved Viking figures, five Valkyries attend two knights. The Valkyries are each posed differently—reflecting the fascinating variety of the Vikings' death myths.

popular with the Frankish nobles in the ninth century.

The Gokstad ship is so well preserved that it can be studied as a model of a Viking ship of the time, and it explains why the Vikings were able to control the seas and rivers from the Baltic to the Bosporus. As an example of shipbuilding and naval architecture, it was centuries ahead of the vessels of other lands. The Gokstad ship was an open vessel made of oak, 76 feet 6 inches long overall, 17 feet 6 inches wide, and just under 6 feet 5 inches deep from keel to gunwale. It had a normal draft of about 3 feet and an equal freeboard (the distance between the gunwale and the water line). The mast was partly cut off when the ship was buried, but experts estimate that it was originally between 37 and 41 feet tall. The sides of the vessel were pierced with holes for sixteen pairs of oars. Since there are no thwarts for oarsmen to sit on, it is assumed that they sat on their sea chests.

Below the gunwale was a shield rack; thirty-three shields, painted alternately black and yellow, were found along each rail of the Gokstad ship, from the bow to the stern. These shields were part of the furnishings of the ship, not the personal shields of the crew. They were hung outside the ship, two for each oar hole and each shield overlapping the next. This display of shields was for a vessel in harbor, to "dress up" the ship or identify its owner. Despite many modern pictures that show Viking ships breasting the waves with shields over the gunwale, it was not common practice to shield ships at sea, and one saga derides a chieftain who did this. The shields would have interfered with the handling of the ship and were not often needed as defensive armor because the early Vikings did little fighting at sea.

The keel of the Gokstad ship was carved from a single timber. The vessel was clinker-built, that is, the planks of the hull, called strakes, overlapped each other, and the joints were calked with animal hair dipped in tar. An unusual construction feature was that the strakes below the water line were tied to the ribs with lengths of spruce root, although the rest of the ship was joined with wooden pins. The reason for this method of fastening the planking to the ribs was disclosed when an exact copy of the Gokstad ship was built and sailed across the Atlantic in 1893. The tied strakes gave the vessel flexibility, so it could yield to the movements of the waves. It snaked through the water like a sea serpent. At times the gunwale twisted as much as six inches out of line, but the vessel remained watertight.

Although the bow of the vessel in this painting is like that of the Oseberg ship, the shield rows are reminiscent of the Gokstad ship.

The rudder of the Gokstad ship was a single piece of oak fastened to the right side of the ship, not at the stern, but close to it. A bar attached to the top of the rudder came across the ship and was used to turn the rudder. This type of rudder had several advantages over the more common stern rudder. It could be handled by one man with little effort in the heaviest seas; its position helped prevent drift to leeward when the vessel was sailing across the wind; it created little drag, compared to a stern rudder; and its position on the ship made possible the high sweeping stern that prevented the vessel from taking water in a following sea.

Ships much bigger than the Gokstad ship are described in the sagas, but even these could not have carried over forty men. Traditionally the most famous of the big ships was the *Long Serpent* of King Olaf Tryggvesson, which had sixty-eight oars; there were others as large or larger—but they were all built after the year 1000. It is probable that these were battleships, designed to fight at sea, rather than raiding ships. The basic raiding ship was probably not much larger than the Gokstad ship of thirty-two oars.

Viking ships were the fastest things afloat in their day, and for many years after. They were the most seaworthy vessels of the age, the only vessels that could safely cope with the perils of the open sea. Shallow in draft and light in weight, they could be rowed up rivers or hauled over portages. The Viking ships permitted the adventurous Northman to go *i viking* and to dominate much of Europe for more than two centuries. Then they carried him for the first time beyond the rim of his hemisphere to the shores of a new world.

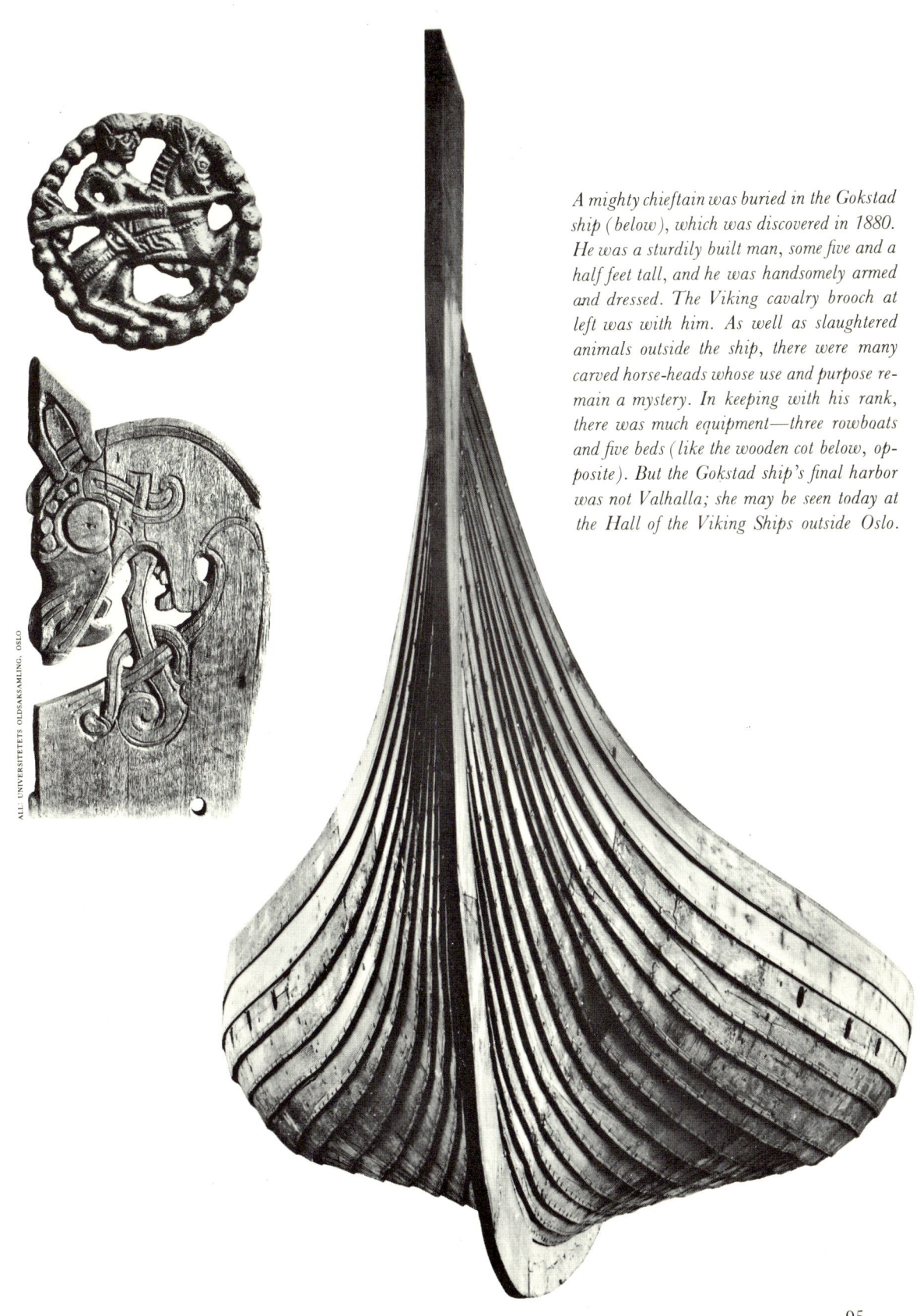

A mighty chieftain was buried in the Gokstad ship (below), which was discovered in 1880. He was a sturdily built man, some five and a half feet tall, and he was handsomely armed and dressed. The Viking cavalry brooch at left was with him. As well as slaughtered animals outside the ship, there were many carved horse-heads whose use and purpose remain a mystery. In keeping with his rank, there was much equipment—three rowboats and five beds (like the wooden cot below, opposite). But the Gokstad ship's final harbor was not Valhalla; she may be seen today at the Hall of the Viking Ships outside Oslo.

95

BODLEIAN LIBRARY, OXFORD

96

VI

EXPLORERS AND COLONISTS

Not all the Vikings who left their homelands behind them sailed for loot or plunder. There were many traders who sought to open up new markets; and there were many who would today be called explorers, men attracted by the lure of far-off places. Ottar of Norway was one such Viking rover, and Alfred the Great added an account of his voyaging to the translation he made of the history of the world.

Ottar described to King Alfred his life in the far north; he talked of his reindeer herds and the tribute he received from the Finns in bearskins, bird feathers, and walrus teeth and hides. He explained that the hides were most important, for a strong, useful rope was made from them. Ottar also spoke about the great trade route along the southern coast of Denmark, and he gave Alfred the first accurate and thorough account of the geography of the Northland.

But Ottar was a curious seaman as well as a trader. He wanted to know what, if anything, was in the wasteland to the north of his country. Sailing north for three days he passed the farthest point to which the whale hunters normally went. For three more days he sailed along a rugged coast; then the land turned east. Ottar waited for a westerly wind and sailed before it for four days until the coastline turned south. Again he waited for a favorable wind, which carried him southward for five days to the mouth of a river. So far all had been barren land, but here there were people. Since they did not seem friendly, Ottar went home. Later, he visited England and gave Alfred the first eyewitness account of the arctic.

Ottar's voyage did not prove anything or reveal anything of value at that time. It merely satisfied his curiosity. He had rounded Europe's most northerly point, North

A carved head from the Oseberg ship stares out as if at strange lands.

Three sailors in a Viking ship smaller than the sea monster beneath it spy land ahead. The vivid illustration is from a twelfth-century manuscript.

Cape, sailed through that part of the Arctic Ocean called the Barents Sea, and then headed south through the White Sea to the mouth of either the Dvina or the Onega River in northern Russia. The Barents Sea is now named for the Dutch explorer Willem Barents—who "discovered" it seven hundred years after Ottar sailed through it. The trip has been made many times since by sturdy whalers and rugged Russian icebreakers. But Ottar sailed in an open boat —similar to a large rowboat—with one small sail controlled by walrus-hide ropes.

Some of the Viking voyages of exploration were deliberate; some were made at the whim of the winds. Gales that carried the ships far off course were responsible for the first two Viking visits to Iceland. When the voyagers gave a good account of the vast island, a third Norwegian Viking, Floki, set out to explore it. He is said to have used the same means to find it that Noah supposedly used to determine when the flood had subsided. Floki carried three ravens which he released at intervals. The first two birds returned to perch in the rigging. When the third did not come back, he followed the direction it had taken until he sighted the mountains of Iceland. Floki wintered on the island, where he was battered by icy storms until spring came. Understandably, he called the place Iceland.

A few years later, in 874, two foster brothers, Leif and Ingolf, were on a Viking raid with three young nobles. On the way home to Norway a fight started in which the foster brothers killed two of the boys. For this, Leif, who caused the fatal quarrel, was outlawed in Norway—which meant the loss of all his possessions. He and his brother decided to emigrate to Iceland, and they sailed to the island to look it over. Pleased with what they found, Ingolf returned to Norway to prepare for the move while Leif made a quick raid to Ireland. He returned with enough plunder to finance the venture and twelve Irish slaves to help with the work.

The brothers set out in two ships with household goods, cattle, their wives and relatives, and a small band of freemen. Ingolf took with him the pillars of the high seat in his hall, which were carved with sacred Viking images. When he neared the coast of Iceland, he cast these overboard, vowing to settle wherever the gods caused them to drift onto the beach. The gods made a good choice by washing the pillars ashore near Iceland's present capital, Reykjavik.

Leif, who may have learned something of Christianity in Ireland, would have nothing to do with this pagan practice, and he landed independently of Ingolf. The site of

The first voyager to Iceland may have been a sixth-century Irish monk named Brendan, seen below with a boatload of fellow monks. But Iceland's first colonizer was the Viking Ingolf Arnarson, above.

When the Vikings first glimpsed the snow-covered peaks of Iceland, the land must have appeared grim. But much of the island is fertile, with flowering lakesides (above) and fields rich in volcanic soil.

Leif's landing is unknown, for his Irish slaves soon revolted, murdered the Vikings, and fled with the women to a small neighboring island. Here Ingolf found them, killed the slaves, reclaimed the women, and delivered a sermon on the folly of those who did not respect the ancient gods. This is the legendary account of the colonization of Iceland. Some of it may stem from the imagination of the story teller; but there is no doubt that Leif and Ingolf were real.

Iceland's first Viking colonists were quickly followed by others. An early Icelandic account of the settlement of the island lists the names of four hundred of the original settler-chieftains and about twenty-five hundred of their followers. And by the year 930 there were at least twenty thousand people in the new land. Historians have long debated the reason for this mass migration. Some say it was caused by the harsh rule of Harold Fairhair, who had conquered all of Norway at about that time. But others point out that many of the early colonists had been on Harold's side in the decisive battle that gained him the throne, and that many other settlers were Vikings from Ireland and Scotland who had not been persecuted by Harold.

It is more probable that most of the rugged, independent Northmen went to Iceland for the same reasons that early colonists came to North America—to obtain land and to find freedom and equality. They came to farm, not to fight or plunder, although many of them later went *i viking* to Ireland, England, and the Continent.

They settled in small groups of families scattered widely around the coastline of the island. There was not enough tillable land to raise crops, but there was good pasturage. The Icelanders raised sheep and some cattle but depended on hunting and fishing for most of their food. Living conditions were primitive. In the recently excavated home of one prominent colonist named Njal only a few iron

At the left of the road in this photograph are the stark cliffs that form the flank of the famous Law Mount, where Iceland's ancient lawgivers assembled. On the right side of the road is the Plain of the Parliament, a landscape of grass and lava where the Icelandic Althing first gathered in the year 930.

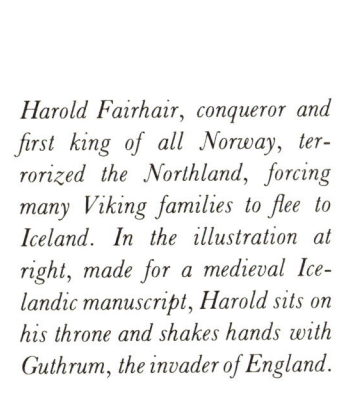

Harold Fairhair, conqueror and first king of all Norway, terrorized the Northland, forcing many Viking families to flee to Iceland. In the illustration at right, made for a medieval Icelandic manuscript, Harold sits on his throne and shakes hands with Guthrum, the invader of England.

tools were found; the remaining hammers and other utensils were made of stone. There was no pottery, but there was a clay-lined trough for use as a bathtub—a refinement of civilization that was rare in the empire of Charlemagne or the kingdom of Alfred.

Iceland was not a colony of Norway. It was an independent country until the year 1264. At first it had no government; there was no king or overlord. All of the landowners were equal and fiercely independent. It soon became evident that some form of organization was necessary to settle disputes in a more practical manner than blood feuds. This led to the formation of *godords*—associations of neighboring landowners who selected their most prominent member as the *godi*, or chieftain. Any power that the *godi* exerted was probably through persuasion since he had no civil authority, although he was also the temple priest and presided over religious ceremonies. Soon disputes arose between neighboring *godords*, and since there was no central authority to control them, the strongest of the groups could make themselves the law and mete out their own justice. In order to put a stop to the resulting disorder, the Althing, an all-island parliament, was formed. It met, almost without interruption, from the year 930 until 1798. Not since the days of ancient Greece had there been such an effective democratic government.

The Althing sent one member to Norway to study that country's laws and frame a code for Iceland. Another delegate surveyed the island to find a suitable meeting place

101

Running down the middle of the manuscript page at right are pairs of warriors locked in combat. This page is from the great fourteenth-century collection of tales about Viking kings and Icelandic heroes known as the Flatey Book. These stories were recited and developed over the centuries by the poets of Iceland. The evocative painting at left by Schiott shows a saga reading in an Icelandic farmhouse.

and selected a site about thirty miles east of present-day Reykjavik. It was called the *Thingvellir*—the Plain of the Parliament. It is today, as it was then, a five-mile-long green plain on a riverbank from which a grassy slope rises to the foot of a rock cliff. The thingmen, or legislators, sat on this slope, and at its top was the *Logberg*—the Law Mount.

All freemen who were landowners could vote in the annual meetings of the Althing, which were a cross between a New England town meeting and a state fair. Anyone could attend the assembly, whether they participated or were merely spectators. The thingmen brought their families and retainers and set up tents or booths on the plain below the slope. Here, between meetings of the congress, there were games, gossip, and sports, and at night the sagas were told and retold around the fires.

The Althing made laws and served as a court of justice, but its great weakness was that it had no executive power—it could not enforce the laws it made or its judicial decisions. Most of the fiery Vikings were not likely to take an adverse judgment calmly, and they often resorted to their own bloody methods of settling disputes. Dueling was one of the traditional ways of solving disagreements.

There were two types of duels. One was the *einvigi*, in which the combatants were allowed to use any weapons they pleased and fight in any manner they saw fit. The *einvigi* was usually to the death. The more common method

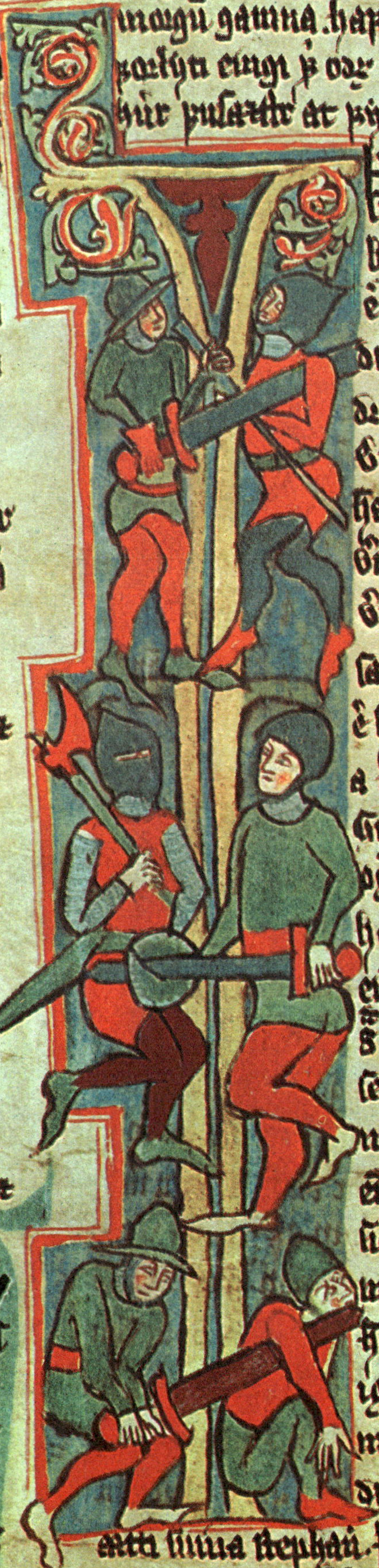

was the *holmganga*, a formal duel with rigid rules. In this type of dueling, a cloak or a skin was staked out on the ground, and a square was marked out with stones on the ground around it. The fight started on the cloak, and neither combatant was allowed to step outside of the square.

Each contestant had a sword of equal length and was allowed three shields. One shield at a time was held for him by a shield man. The man who had been challenged struck first. When a shield was broken, another could be substituted for it until all three were smashed. Then the shieldless contestant had to return to the cloak, if he had left it, and continue to fight without a shield. If a man was wounded so that his blood fell onto the cloak, he could call off the duel without losing his honor.

Christianity came to Iceland gradually and with unique difficulties. For the first century of the Viking occupation, the island was entirely pagan except for a few individuals

One of the greatest Icelandic sagas tells of a series of vengeful family feuds that were only brought to a close when the farm of a heroic lawyer named Njal was set afire. In 1951 the site, called Burnt Njal, was excavated (photo at far left) and metal objects were found that support the chronology of the saga; apparently the farm was burned in 1011. Other Icelandic artifacts are shown on these pages. At left above is a hoard of coins from many countries, confirming that the Vikings were far-ranging traders. Below the coins are spears, a sword, and a fragment of ring armor dating from before 1000—the oldest collection yet found on the island. The two handsome swords and the scabbard tip above are from about the same time; like most Icelandic weapons, they were manufactured in Norway or Denmark.

Three of Iceland's early bishops were later canonized. Above, in a fifteenth-century tapestry, they are served by two solemn assistants.

who had been baptized while *i viking*, either for reasons of faith or because it was good for business. Then, around the middle of the tenth century, twelve Irish monks arrived in Iceland to preach Christianity. They followed in the wake of some of their brethren who had voyaged to Iceland as early as 825 and had lived in that land as hermits. But with the coming of the Vikings, these few monks had sailed away. The twelve Irish monks were not successful in their mission, for they were unable to make any converts. Then in 981, a widely traveled Icelander who had become a Christian came home with a Saxon bishop. They preached zealously and made some converts, but when newly baptized Christians stopped paying their dues for the upkeep of the pagan temples, these two missionaries were banished from Iceland.

At the end of the tenth century, Olaf Tryggvesson was king of Norway, and he was a militant Christian. Desiring to convert the Icelanders, he sent out a missionary who immediately after his arrival started to pull down temples and smash images; he was promptly thrown off the island. Olaf's first missionary was followed by a second who, for a while, was more successful, making many converts—and many enemies. When he too was banished, King Olaf was so incensed that he ordered some pagan Icelanders who were visiting Norway to be executed. Two prominent islanders who were in Norway interceded for the victims and promised to try to convert their countrymen if Olaf would let them go.

These two islanders, Gizur the White and his son-in-law Hjalti, returned to Iceland in the year 1000 with several priests. Instead of trying to make converts they marched into the meeting of the Althing and demanded the right to demonstrate a Christian mass. By this time there was a sizable Christian minority from previous missionary efforts, and these people took the position that if the Althing would not permit open discussion of religion they were ready to take up arms in order to be heard. As a result a mass was said on the *Logberg* on Good Friday, followed by a long and bitter debate. Finally the Althing voted to adopt Christianity as Iceland's state religion and ordered all pagans to be baptized—the only time that a country ever adopted Christianity through a democratic process.

The Althing continued to rule the violent country firmly but fairly. Its most serious sentence was the outlawing of an offender. For a minor offense he was banished for three years; for a major crime the banishment was for life, and the victim lost all his possessions and could be killed by anyone who found him. The most famous Viking to be outlawed was Eric the Red. He had come to Iceland when his father was banished from Norway. Then Eric murdered a man, and he in turn was outlawed from Iceland. He decided to go to a new land—Greenland—that had been sighted almost a century before but never explored. Crossing what is now called Denmark Strait, Eric rounded Greenland's southern tip (Cape Farewell), and spent the winter there. In the spring he sailed up a fjord that took him into the most fertile country on the island's west coast. Returning to Iceland, he began to gather settlers for a colony in the new land. To encourage recruits he gave the subarctic island the attractive name it still bears.

In the year 985 Eric sailed off to Greenland with twenty-five boatloads of colonists; but only fourteen ships arrived safely. And the colonists soon found that little was green in the new land. The permanent icecap that covered most of the island left only a narrow strip of land on the west coast that would support life. There, along the edges of the fjords, was enough grass to feed their hungry cattle. The people eked out an existence barely above survival by hunting whales, seals, bear, and reindeer, and by fishing. They discovered iron and made primitive knives, nails, and fish hooks—but, without wood and with little other fuel, they had difficulty smelting the iron. The colony survived on

TEXT CONTINUED ON PAGE 110

Before Christianity was firmly established in Iceland, about 1000, a pagan artist made this statuette of the Viking god Thor holding a strangely shaped sword or hammer.

On this brilliant fifteenth-century map, Greenland ("Gronelanth") is shown north of Iceland and connected to northern Eu

rope by means of Lapland ("Pillappelanth"). The golden streak running down the spine of Greenland indicates glaciers.

ICELANDIC AIRLINES

As whales spout and a lookout at the masthead watches for shoals, Eric the Red's ship moves into a Greenland fjord in the modern drawing below. Eric's son Leif, who discovered America, stands at left; the statue was given to Iceland by the United States.

TEXT CONTINUED FROM PAGE 107

these inhospitable shores for more than four centuries, trading walrus tusks and hides and bearskins and sealskins for the grain they could not grow.

Greenland became a Norwegian colony in the thirteenth century, at the same time as Iceland, and trading with both islands became a monopoly of the Norwegian Crown. For many years a ship was sent out from Norway annually. But, sometime in the early fifteenth century, the ships stopped coming, and the colony died out. The end is still a mystery. One theory is that the usually peaceful Eskimos of the arctic may have attacked the settlers; another is that the climate may have become more rigorous through the years and killed what little vegetation there was. It is thought that as a result, the colonists slowly died of malnutrition. In the Greenland graves studied by archaeologists, the skeletons witness to men under five feet tall and women little more than four feet.

Before the colony in Greenland disappeared, it produced the most famous of all Viking adventurers, Leif

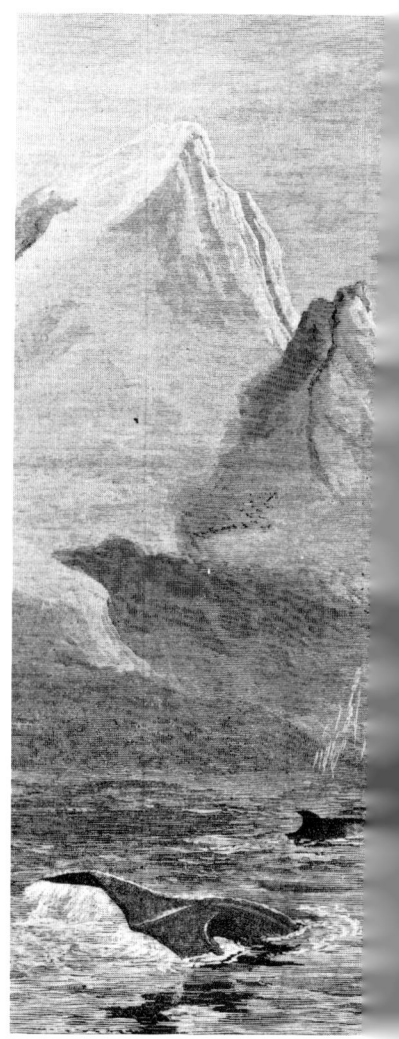

Ericson, son of Eric the Red. Leif's fame rests on two accomplishments. The lesser known one was the conversion of Greenland to Christianity. In the year 999 he journeyed to Norway to the court of Olaf Tryggvesson. The zealous king converted Leif and induced him to return to Greenland with a priest to spread the faith. Although Leif made many converts to Christianity, his pagan father would have none of it. The crusty old outlaw separated himself from his wife when she became a Christian, and he swore that the worst day in Greenland's history was when his son brought back the priest.

But Leif's independent spirit could not be restrained. This Christian Viking sailed forth to his greatest accomplishment—the discovery of the New World.

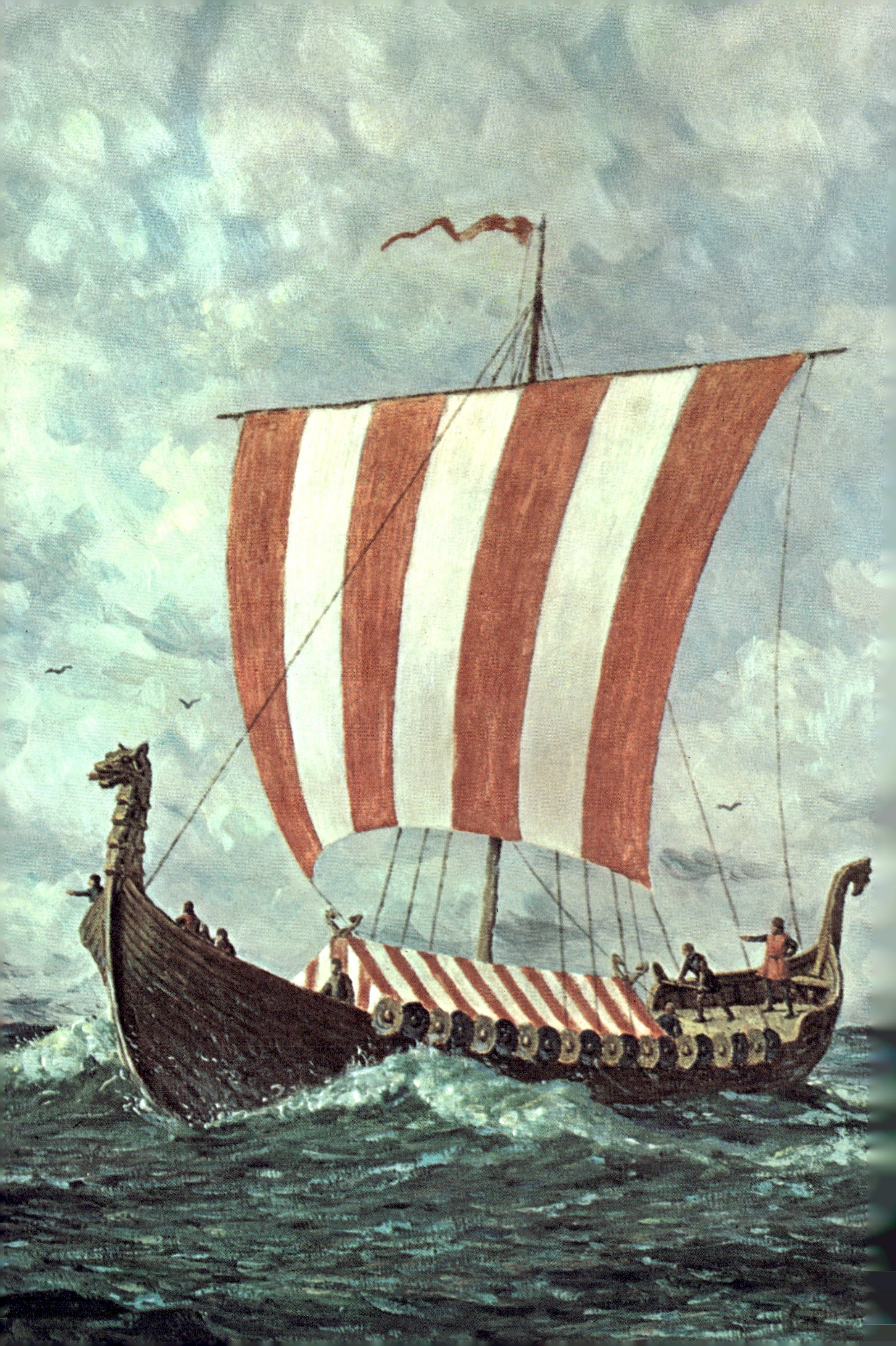

VII

WINELAND THE GOOD

For centuries, historians of Europe and America have waged a scholarly debate. Was the Viking discovery of America history or legend? The story of the voyages of Leif Ericson and his fellow Northmen to the New World is told in detail in two sagas. But were the sagas fact or fiction? To those who defended the view that the Vikings did discover America long before Columbus, it was maddeningly frustrating that no incontrovertible evidence could be found to confirm the sagas, despite endless search. There were many finds—but they all turned out to be either false alarms or mysteries. It seemed as though there would never be a final answer.

Then in the fall of 1963 there was a dramatic break in the case. Some daily newspapers headlined that an explorer had found Leif Ericson's house in Newfoundland. Careful scientists are not yet willing to endorse the Leif Ericson part of the headlines. But there is no question that the Norwegian explorer Dr. Helge Ingstad has discovered ruins that are unmistakably Viking and that predate the voyage of Columbus by almost five hundred years.

After three expeditions during which he surveyed the Atlantic coast of North America by boat and by plane, and with the help of an ancient map, Dr. Ingstad settled on the northern tip of the island of Newfoundland as the most likely site for the settlement described in the sagas. Here, on his fourth expedition, he discovered the ruins of nine structures and a primitive smithy near the fishing village of L'Anse aux Meadows. Only the remains of beaten earthen floors, the outlines of turf walls, and fireplaces with ember pits remain, plus some scraps of iron and a stone anvil. But one of the houses had a great hall in the Viking

TEXT CONTINUED ON PAGE 116

Leif Ericson's men see the American coast in Emil Biorn's painting at left. Above is another Viking who voyaged to America, Thorfinn Karlsefni.

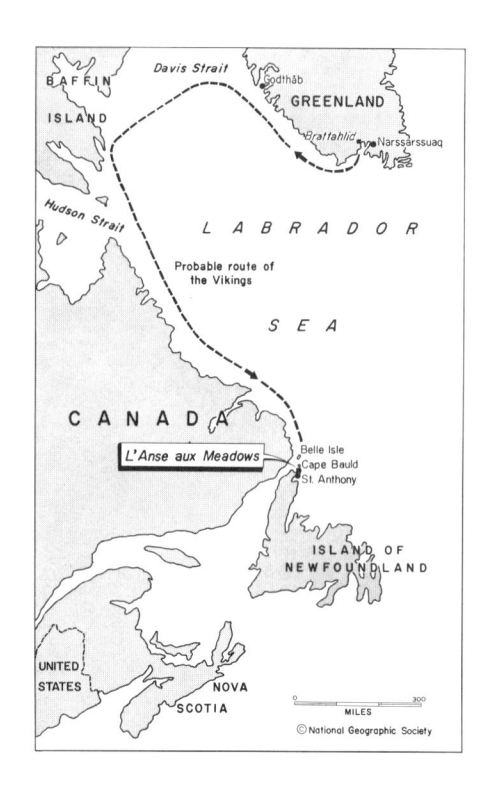

ALL: COPYRIGHT 1963, NATIONAL GEOGRAPHIC SOCIETY

LEIF'S TURNING POINT

Off the Canadian coast the northern tip of Newfoundland sticks up like the proverbial sore thumb; this cape is an obvious turning point for any voyager sailing south along the coast of North America (see map at far left). Thus Dr. Helge Ingstad suspected that the cape would have been a logical place for Leif Ericson to make his camp—a site that Leif and other Vikings could easily find again on subsequent voyages. At L'Anse aux Meadows, a small village on the cape, this hunch was proved correct; traces of a Viking settlement were found. Below at left, Dr. Ingstad carefully removes dirt from a fireplace constructed like the hearths of the Northland; at right his assistants dig a precise ditch, hoping to unearth Viking relics (a few nails have been found, but much has been destroyed by the soil's extreme acidity). At left a scientist stands on the fenced-off foundation of one of the houses in the settlement that may have been built by Leif five hundred years before Columbus' voyage.

TEXT CONTINUED FROM PAGE 113

style, and the ember pits were typically Norse. The buildings were not structurally or stylistically similar to those built by Indians or Eskimos; furthermore, the natives had no knowledge of iron smelting.

Radiocarbon dating of charcoal from the ember pits indicates that the site was occupied around the year 1000, but there is nothing to prove that the structures were built by Leif Ericson. Yet they were built by some Viking at exactly the time when the sagas say that Leif landed on the coast of North America.

The two books of sagas that tell the story of the early Viking voyages to America are the Flatey Book, which was written in the late fourteenth century, and Hauk's Book, which was written in the early years of the same century. Both were based on earlier manuscripts, since lost; and the manuscripts, in turn, were based on even earlier oral renditions of the sagas. The stories in the two works are parallel in most essentials but disagree in many details. The most important difference is that in the Flatey Book Leif is not the actual discoverer of America; the credit for first sighting the New World belongs to a Northman named Bjarni Herjulfson. If this saga is true, Bjarni is the world's most unsung hero—and his lack of fame is due to his filial piety.

Bjarni was a sea-roving trader for most of the year, but he always came home to spend the winter with his father in Iceland. When he returned one year, he found that his father had moved to Greenland. Without unloading his ship Bjarni set out to follow. He had never been to Greenland, but people told him that it had a coast cut by fjords and backed by tall, snow-covered mountains. He was sure he would know it when he saw it.

All went well for three days. Then a fog closed in and the ship drifted. When the sun came out, Bjarni's crew spread sail and went on, not knowing now where they were. Soon they sighted land, but there were no fjords or mountains. Bjarni turned north and sailed for two more days. When they again sighted land, the crew wanted to go ashore for wood and water, but Bjarni said, "That is not Greenland," and sailed on. Three days later they made a third landfall, and again the stubborn Icelander refused to stop. Finally the wind changed direction, and after running before a gale from the south for four days, they saw in the distance snow-capped mountains. "They directed their course thither and landed in the evening below a cape on which there was a boat, and there upon this cape dwelt

An American artist drew this view of Leif's fleet of ships sailing close-hauled toward the New World.

Herjulf, Bjarni's father. Bjarni now went to his father, gave up his voyaging, and remained with his father while Herjulf lived." So ends the saga of the man so dedicated to finding his father that he had no eyes for the New World.

Although Bjarni was not curious about the new land he had sighted, Leif Ericson was. He bought Bjarni's boat, gathered a crew of thirty-five men, and in the year 1002 set out to backtrack on Bjarni's voyage. He first came to Bjarni's third landfall:

There they sailed up to the land, and having cast anchor and lowered a boat, went ashore and saw no grass there. The background was all great glaciers, and the intermediate land from the sea to the glaciers was like one flat rock, and the country seemed to them destitute of value. Then Leif said, 'We have not failed to land, like Bjarni; now I will give this country a name and call it Helluland' [the land of flat stone]. Thereupon they returned on board, after which they sailed to sea and discovered the second land. Again they sailed up to the land and lowered a boat and went ashore. This land was low-lying and wooded, and wherever they went there were wide stretches of white sand, and the slope from the sea was not abrupt. Then Leif said, 'This land shall be given a name from its resources and shall be called Markland' [woodland]. After which they returned to the ship as

This Icelandic map shows Leif's three landfalls, Helleland, Markland, and Vinland ("Winlandie"). The promontory that terminates in Vinland bears a close resemblance to Newfoundland's long cape. Because the Viking name for Indians was skraellings, *the region south of Markland is "Skralinge Land."*

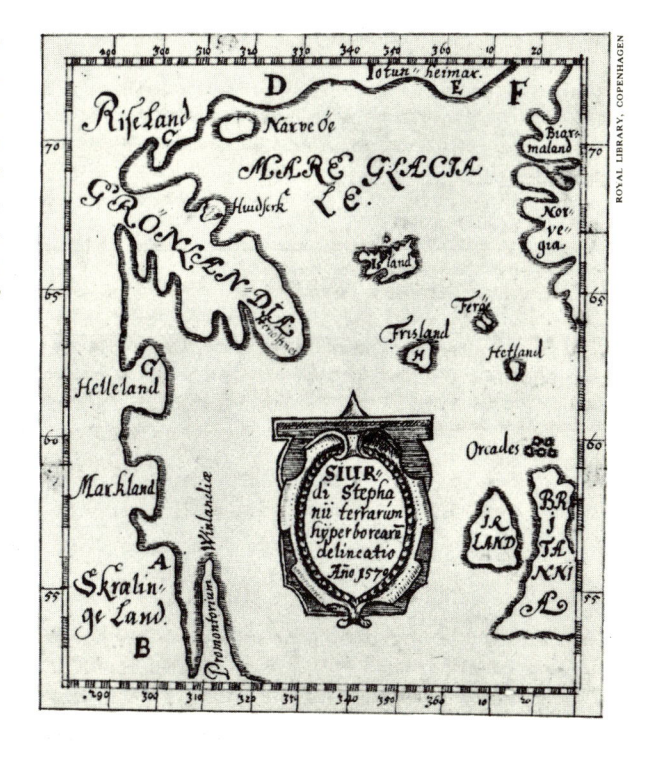

quickly as possible. And they sailed after that in the open sea with a northeast wind and were out two days before they saw land, toward which they sailed and . . . cast anchor, and carrying their leather kitbags ashore, they put up shelters; but, later on, deciding to pass the winter there, they made large houses.

The third landfall had brought them to a fine country in which salmon, game, and grass were plentiful. Leif split the party into two groups, one half to explore the land, while the other kept camp. One day a German member of the crew named Tyrkir failed to return with the exploring party. Leif organized a manhunt, and the missing German was soon found in a very happy mood. He had discovered something he was quite fond of—grapes. Then Leif said to his crew, " 'Now we will do two things. We will gather grapes and cut down vines and fell wood to make a cargo for my ship.' So a cargo [of timber] was cut for the ship, and in the spring they made ready and sailed away; and Leif gave the country a name according to its resources, and called it Wineland. [Vinland]"

When Leif returned to Greenland, his brother Thorvald felt that a larger area should have been explored, so Leif gave him Bjarni's ship for another voyage. With thirty men, Thorvald returned to Leif's camp in Vinland, and after wintering there they explored the neighboring region during the first summer, finding no sign of habitation except a wooden grain-holder. During the next summer they explored the coast in the ship. They found a beautiful headland on which Thorvald said he would like to make his home.

As they were returning to the ship from inspecting this spot they saw on the beach three lumps that turned out to be canoes; under each of the canoes were three *skraellings*—the Northmen's name for Eskimos, and the name they also applied to American Indians. "Thereupon they divided their party and laid hands on all of them except one who escaped with his canoe. They killed the eight and afterwards went back to the headland where they saw inside the fjords some mounds, which they took to be dwelling places."

It was most unfortunate for Thorvald that one Indian got away. The next morning the bay was covered with Indians in canoes. The Northmen set their shields over the side of their ship and withstood the attack, and the Indians left after discharging a few flights of arrows. Thorvald was the only casualty, with an arrow in his side. He told his crew to leave "after carrying me to that headland which I thought the best place to dwell in. Maybe it was the truth

TEXT CONTINUED ON PAGE 122

The grapes that Tyrkir found and pointed out to Leif (above) were probably misnamed in the saga. Dr. Ingstad and other modern scholars believe the "grapes" were grasses.

The first known reference to Vinland in European histories is at left, a page from Adam of Bremen's eleventh-century manuscript. The word is in the seventh line. Below is a statue of Leif by A. S. Calder. This heroic bronze is notable for accurate detail of dress.

Grasping a thwart-ship tiller, Leif Ericson points to North America. The Norwegian artist Christian Krohg shou

...eif as a portly but salty figure. On the way home, Leif salvaged a cargo of lumber and won the nickname Leif the Lucky.

TEXT CONTINUED FROM PAGE 118

that came into my mouth that I should stay there awhile. Bury me there with a cross at my head and at my feet, and call it Crossness hereafter forever." And thus Thorvald was buried in the New World's first Viking grave.

The next attempted voyage to the New World was by a third son of Eric the Red, Thorstein, who wanted to bring back his brother's body. Still using Bjarni's old boat, he sailed with his wife Gudrid and twenty-five men. This voyage was ill-fated from the start. They tossed about in the open sea all summer and finally returned to another part of Greenland, where Thorstein died.

Several summers passed. It was not until 1009 that the next expedition set out for America. This was headed by an Icelander, Thorfinn Karlsefni, who came to Greenland to trade, spent the winter with Leif Ericson, and married Thorstein's widow. Throughout the long cold months the stories of the adventures of Leif and his brothers excited Thorfinn's interest, and in the spring he sailed for the New World. This was by far the largest expedition, numbering 160 men. The three ships also carried cattle, and women went along for the first time, including Gudrid and Eric the Red's daughter Freydis, a strong-willed woman who was married to a weakling named Thorvard.

Their first two landfalls were made in a country much like Leif had described, and they concluded that these were the places he had called Helluland and Markland. They continued to sail along the coast for some distance, past long stretches of desolate sands. They had with them a pair of Scottish slaves whom Olaf Tryggvesson had given Leif, telling him they were great runners, swifter than the deer. At the end of the sand dunes they landed these men, with orders to run southward and explore the resources of the country. Three days later the Scots returned bearing grapes and wild wheat and guided the ship to a pleasant bay, which Thorfinn named Straumfjord. The party spent the first summer here, hunting and fishing, and Gudrid had a baby, Snorri.

The winter was more severe than they expected from Leif's reports, and when the pastures were snow-covered, and hunting and fishing petered out, they moved to an island where there was better grazing for the cattle. When they started to feel the pinch of hunger, Thorhall the Hunter, an ill-tempered old companion of Eric the Red, returned to the mainland and disappeared. Three days later they found him lying on a crag chanting incantations. The next day a whale was washed up on the island, and

The Indians encountered by the Vikings in North America used utensils like these: a wide-mouthed pottery jar and a stone axe with a wooden handle; both were found on Massachusetts' eastern shores.

Thorfinn and Gudrid prayerfully observe their arrival in the New World in this romantic drawing. Their colonizing expedition first encamped at Straumfjord, a site not yet identified by researchers but believed to be in New England.

everybody ate heartily until Thorhall said, "Is not the Red Beard [Thor] more useful than your Christ? This is my reward for chanting to my patron Thor." The Christians indignantly tossed the rest of the whale meat over a cliff.

In the spring the grumpy Thorhall, annoyed because they had not found the mountains of wine-making grapes that he had been led to expect, took one ship and nine other disgruntled members of the party and started for home—they ended in Ireland as slaves. With the other two vessels Thorfinn and his followers continued south to a river mouth, which they named Hop. Here there were wild grapes and wheat and streams teeming with fish. Grazing was good and game was plentiful, so they built a permanent camp. About two weeks after their arrival, nine canoes full of Indians entered the river mouth. They stayed for a while, watching the white men, and then paddled off.

The Northmen saw no more of the Indians until the next spring. Then, early one morning, a fleet of canoes appeared, "so many that the sea was black with them." The Indians made signs of peace and the Vikings displayed a white shield to indicate their peaceful intentions. For some time after this they traded with the Indians, bartering red cloth for pelts. The red men wanted to trade for weapons, but Thorfinn would not permit this.

All went well until one day a bull from the Northmen's herd came bellowing out of the woods and charged into the Indians. Terrified, they piled into their canoes and fled, obviously in an angry mood. They were gone for three weeks, during which time the Northmen built a palisade

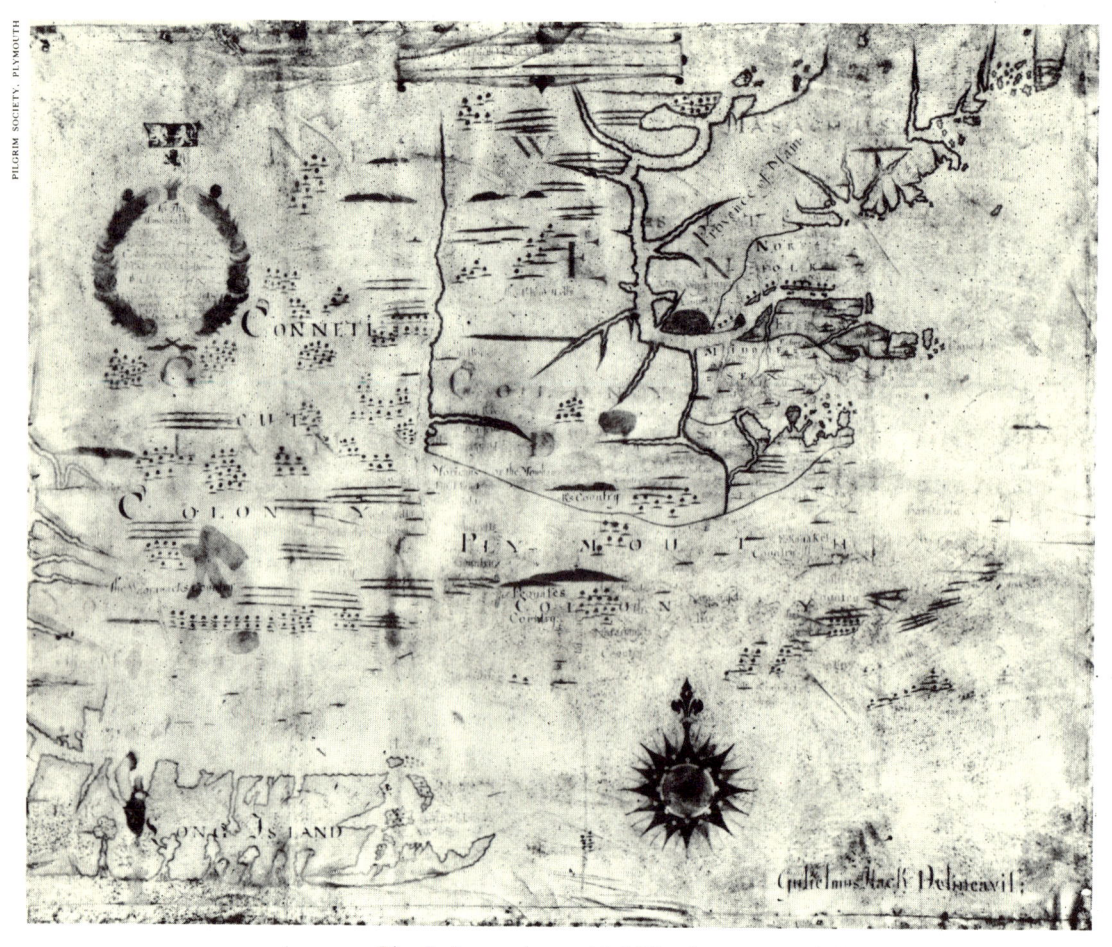

The Indians who troubled Thorfinn were probably early Iroquois (like the brave at right) or Algonquins. During the Viking Era these tribes held most of the coastal territory shown on the seventeenth-century map above.

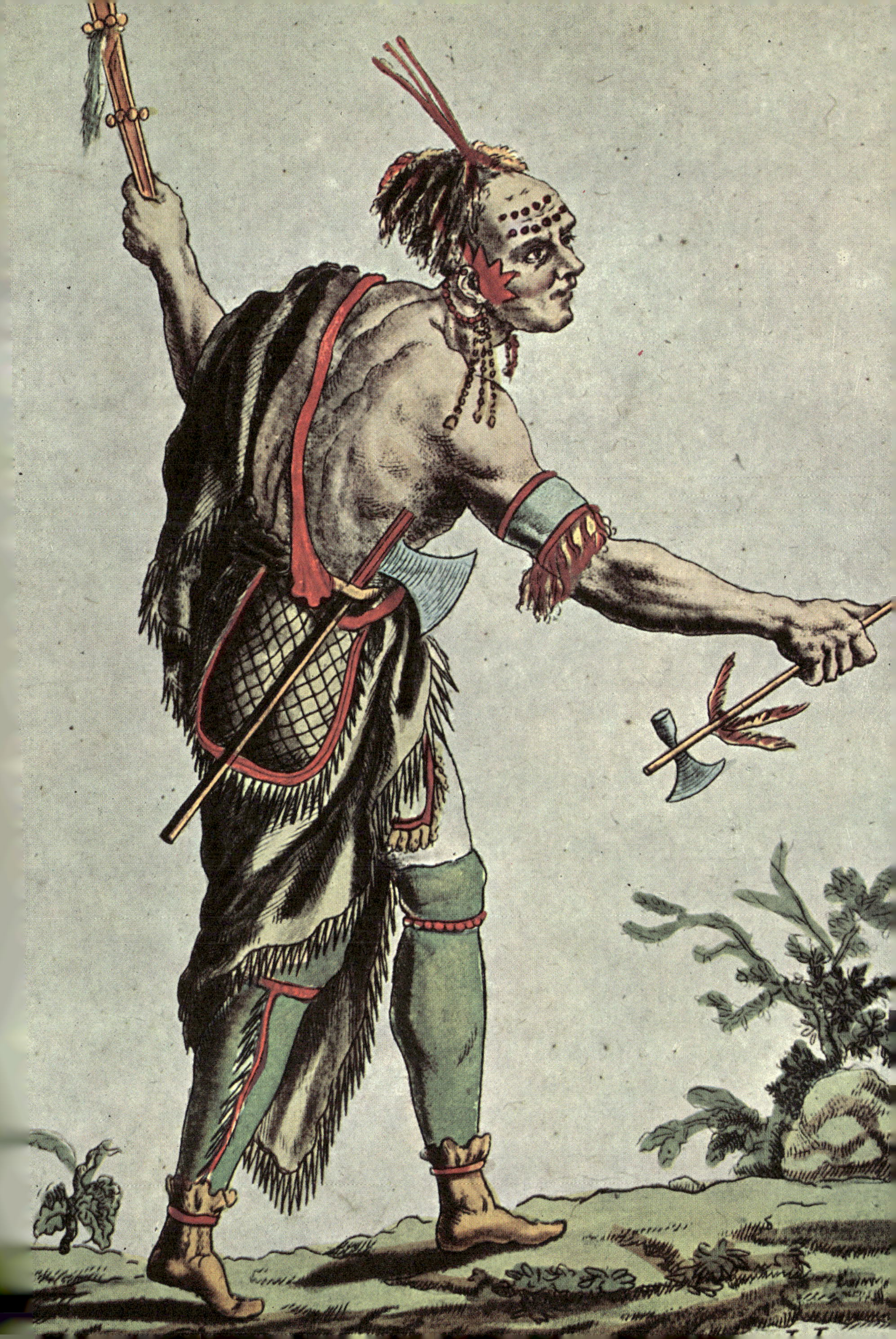

A theory long cherished by enthusiasts of Viking explorations is that a round stone tower in Newport, Rhode Island, was built by Vikings sometime between 1000 and 1500. They point out that the tower (right) bears many similarities to medieval structures in Sweden and Europe—most demonstrably to the Tower of St. Bavo in Belgium. That thirteenth-century tower is also held up by eight stone columns; the masonry of the arch through which St. Bavo is seen in the photograph at left is strikingly like that of the Newport Tower's arches (detail at far right). Unconvinced, historians contend that the Newport Tower is a beacon little more than three centuries old.

around their camp. But when the savages did return they caught the white men outside the stockade. Protected by flights of arrows that darkened the sky, Indians swarmed ashore from their canoes screaming and waving war rattles. The red men also had a novel weapon, "a pole with a very large globe, closely resembling a sheep's pouch and dark in color, and it flew from the pole up on land and over the party and made a terrible noise where it came down. Upon this a great fear came on Thorfinn and his party, so that they wished for nothing but to get away upstream." At this point Eric's daughter Freydis came upon the scene, derided the men as cowards, picked up the sword of a dead Northman, and charged the savages. The Indians panicked at the sight of this long-haired, blond Amazon and made off in their canoes, leaving four dead. The Northmen lost two men.

Thorfinn's purpose was peaceful settlement, and it was evident that this would no longer be possible at Hop. They therefore went back to Straumfjord for the third winter. Here trouble developed among the settlers, principally over the wives of the few married men. Thorfinn decided to give up and return to Greenland. Before leaving they captured two Indian boys who, after they learned to speak Norse, told them of a land "opposite their own where people lived who wore white clothes and uttered loud cries and carried poles and went with flags. It is thought that this was Greater Ireland." This last is a reference to one of several legends of some Irish monks who reached America before the Vikings.

The last voyage to Vinland recorded in detail is that of Freydis, wife of Thorvard. This aggressive female induced two brothers, lately arrived in Greenland from Iceland, to undertake an expedition on shares. The brothers were to take thirty men and some women in their large ship, Freydis and her husband an equal number in their smaller vessel; but Freydis smuggled five extra men aboard. The brothers reached Vinland first and made camp in Leif's house. When Freydis arrived she insisted that they leave, on the grounds that her brother had loaned the house to her.

The brothers and their party made camp nearby, but it was soon apparent that Freydis had no intention of having equality of command in the settlement. She intended to dominate. Things deteriorated to the point that the two camps were not speaking. One morning, very early, Freydis paid a visit to the camp of the brothers. She returned to tell Thorvard that she had gone to buy the larger ship and the brothers had insulted and mistreated her. She induced her weak husband to lead their men against the sleeping neighboring camp, where they overpowered the men and led them out, one by one, and killed them. When Thorvard's men refused to kill the five women in the camp, Freydis grabbed an axe and did this grisly chore herself. Then, after threatening dire consequences to anybody who talked, she loaded the cargo that both camps had been preparing into the larger ship and sailed back to Greenland. Leif Ericson found out about her grim deed later but could not bring himself to punish his sister.

This is the skeleton of the story of the early Viking voyages to America as it is told in the Flatey Book. Hauk's Book does not mention Bjarni and has Leif make his discovery by accident, as Bjarni did in the other version. Until Dr. Ingstad's recent discovery, many serious scholars would not accept these sagas as historical evidence. One who

New Englanders have made several suggestions as to the location of Hop—the second settlement of Thorfinn. To fit the description in the saga, the site must be a pond through which a river runs to the sea. Both sites shown here have those characteristics. At left is a rock at Bass River on Cape Cod that was once bored to receive mooring pins; at right is Dighton Rock, inscribed with mysterious symbols.

held this view said, "The story of the colonization of America by Northmen rests on narratives that are mythological in form and obscure in meaning; ancient yet not contemporary . . . No clear historical evidence establishes the probability that they accomplished the passage, and no vestige of their presence on our continent has been found." Now it can be said, on the basis of archaeological evidence, that this last sentence is no longer true. But even before the recent find, there was a strong historical tradition behind the belief that the Vikings had come to America.

Adam of Bremen, the highly regarded head of the cathedral school at Bremen, mentioned Vinland in his description of the Church's far-flung diocese completed in 1075. He said that King Sweyn of Denmark had told him of the land. Since Sweyn ruled from 1047 to 1075 he could have learned about it from those who had been there. Another early writer, Ari Thorgilsson, also mentions Vinland several times. Ari, the first Icelandic historian, doubtless heard many stories of these famous explorations as he was but two generations removed (1067–1148) from them—and his grandfather was a cousin of Thorfinn's. Ari never described Vinland but merely mentioned it casually, as though everybody who might read his books would be expected to know about it.

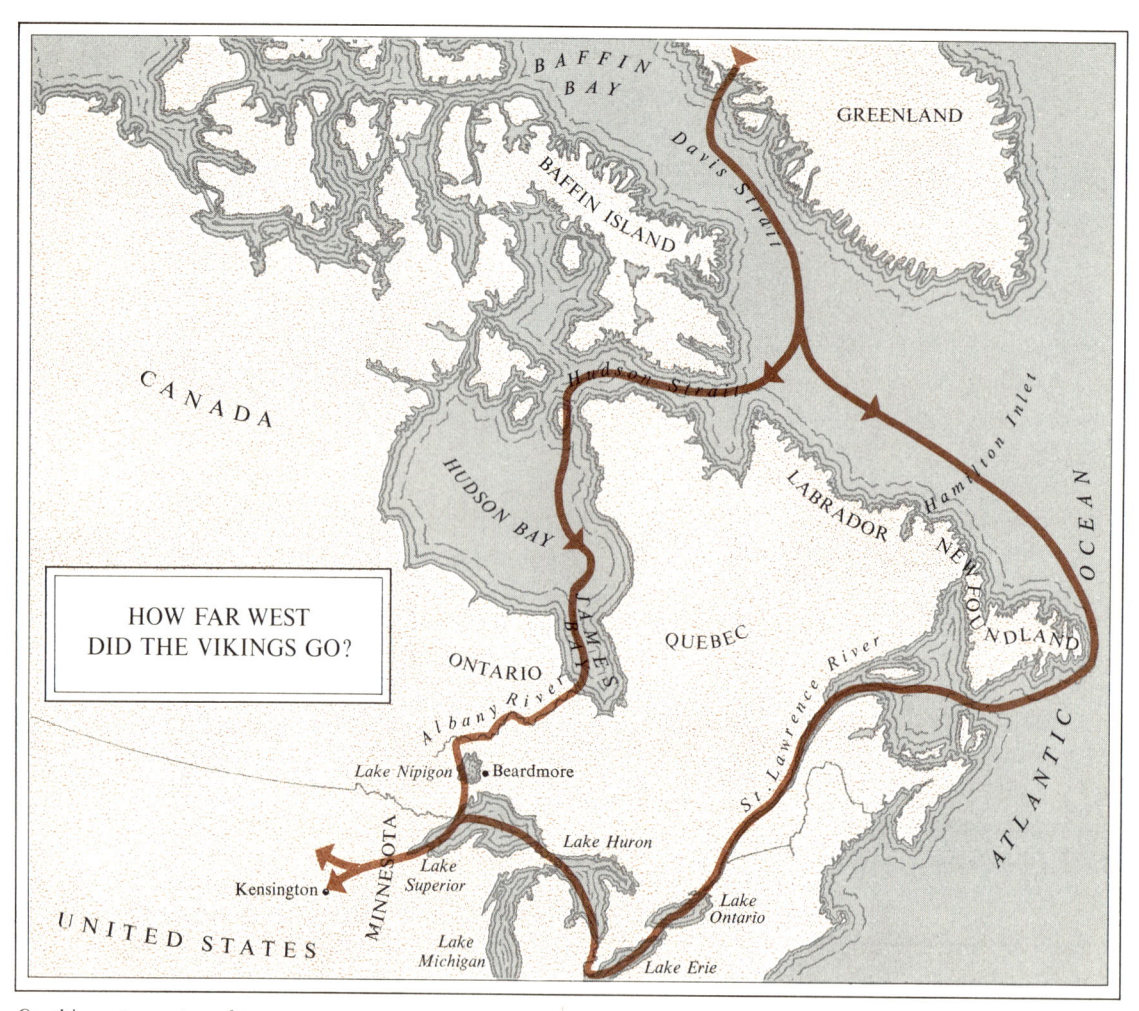

On this map are traced two routes Viking explorers may have taken via rivers and lakes into the heart of the wilderness of North America.

There is another piece of confirming evidence—the mystery weapon of the *skraellings* that the saga describes in their fight with Thorfinn. In a history of Indian tribes in the United States is a description of an identical weapon. It says that the Algonquins "in ancient times constructed a very formidable instrument of attack by sewing up a large boulder in a new skin. To this a long handle was tied and after being painted it assumed the appearance of a solid globe upon a pole. It was borne by several warriors who acted as ballisteers. Brought down upon a group of men of a sudden it produced consternation and death." The Algonquins were a tribe whose lands embraced most of the river-mouth site that Thorfinn had called Hop.

A point made by those who belittle the sagas is that the feats of navigation reported are beyond belief. Both Thorvard and Freydis are said to have sailed to the exact spot where Leif built a house. This aspect of the sagas is possibly an embellishment, but it brings up the greatest Viking mystery. How did they navigate? Perhaps they did not pin-point Leif's house in Vinland, but they regularly sailed across hundreds of miles of open water and hit the small Orkney and Shetland islands and their settlements in Ireland with complete assurance.

Perhaps the Vikings were able to navigate so effectively because they collected and shared such a great wealth of lore on prevailing winds and tides. Also, the Northmen knew something of celestial navigation; the sagas about Leif mention that he recorded the sun's position. And it is thought that they used some kind of primitive astrolabe, forerunner of the sextant, for taking sights on celestial bodies, but there is no record of how this instrument worked. To all of this was probably added the "sixth sense" that has been attributed to ships' captains in sailing ship days to account for the Vikings' ability to get from place to place over the wild and uncharted Atlantic. Adding to the Vikings' known navigational accomplishments, some writers also credit them with having explored the Great Lakes area.

Although Dr. Ingstad's find provides the answer to the big question of whether the Vikings reached America, minor mysteries remain. The greatest of these is the grapes of the sagas. There are no grapes in Newfoundland. For that reason it has generally been believed that Vinland was farther south. The most prevalent opinion has been that Helluland was somewhere in Labrador, or possibly Baffin Island, which is nearer to Greenland. Nova Scotia has been accepted as the most likely site for Markland; with Vinland somewhere between the Gulf of St. Lawrence and Chesapeake Bay. Elaborate cases have been built for several specific locations based on some detail mentioned in the sagas; a faulty process because it is generally agreed that many of the incidents in all the sagas were added to embroider the basically true tale.

There are three possible explanations for the grapes. One is that they were merely an embellishment in the saga. Another, which influenced Dr. Ingstad's thinking, was advanced by a Swedish linguist who said that "wine" might refer to grass rather than wild grapes. The third is an ingenious surmise that Leif might have followed in his father's footsteps in naming his newly discovered land. Eric had named the icy island to which he wanted to attract set-

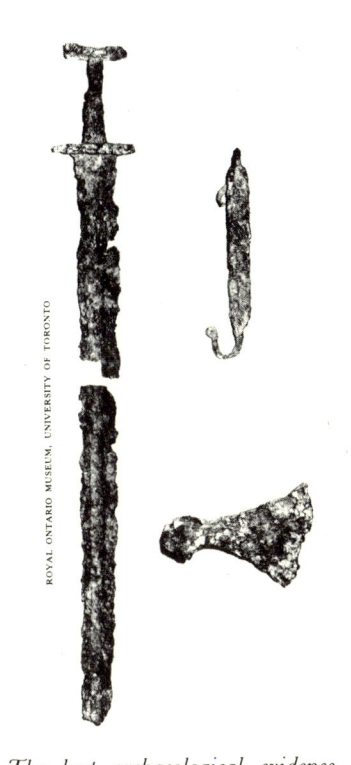

The best archaeological evidence of Viking penetration of the interior of North America are these three pieces of rusted iron found in Beardmore, Ontario, in 1930: a broken sword, an axehead, and an object that has been called a rattle. Experts say they are legitimate relics of the Northland, but whether they were buried with a Viking explorer or brought to America some time later still remains in doubt.

The fourteenth-century Viking halberd below was found not far from the Kensington Stone. The strange medieval tool above was also found in Minnesota. Experts believe neither to be authentic Viking relics.

tlers Greenland. Leif may have reasoned that the heavy drinking Vikings would flock to a place called Wineland.

Many intriguing theories have been advanced regarding possible sites of Viking colonization in the New World; but the theories have usually been based more on local pride than on scientific research. On the east coast of the United States questionable evidences of Viking settlement have been set forth such as a fireplace discovered near the Harvard University campus on the River Charles and an ancient-looking round tower in Newport, Rhode Island (which most experts say was built in Colonial times).

There has been a particularly intensive search to determine whether the Vikings also penetrated America's interior. In this search there have been many false alarms and one interesting puzzle. Several supposed rune stones have turned up in various places and caused some excitement until experts labelled their markings as undecipherable carvings. The puzzle was the Kensington Stone, which was found by a farmer in Minnesota in 1898. This stone—of which there is a replica in the Smithsonian Institution in Washington—bears a runic inscription telling of a western journey of Vikings from Vinland in 1362. Although some scholars condemn it as a forgery, others defend it as genuine.

Whether or not the Vikings reached the Mid-west, as the Kensington Stone proclaims, there is much evidence that they continued to journey to the New World for several hundred years after Leif's voyage. Annals mention two such trips. In the year 1121 a bishop named Eric Gnupsson "sought Wineland". The text does not say whether he reached it or returned. Another writer mentions a vessel which came from Markland to Iceland with a cargo of wood in 1347.

There is other physical evidence which indicates continued commerce with the New World. Some of the graves in Greenland contained coffins of larch wood; and North America is the only logical place from which wood of this tree could have been obtained. And one authentic rune stone was found on Baffin Island in 1824. It said that three Northmen had "raised these marks and cleared ground on the Saturday before Ascension Week, 1135"

The whole story of the Viking voyages to America may never be known, but at long last it is positive that they did set foot in the New World five hundred years before Columbus. And it is very probable that they kept coming—if for no other reason than that they were Vikings.

The controversial Kensington Stone of Minnesota is covered with runic inscriptions on its face (above) and side (right). They tell of a Viking journey from Vinland in 1362 on which ten men were killed by Indians.

133

PHOTO BY SKIRA

134

VIII

THE END OF THE VIKINGS

The voyage of Leif Ericson in the year 1002, which opened the New World to Viking exploration, coincided with the beginning of the end of the Viking Era in the Old World. By this time the Vikings who had established the kingdom of the Rus had become more Russian than Scandinavian. The Vikings who had ravaged France had become the Christian feudal dukes and nobles of Normandy and were now vigorously upholding the Church of which their forebears had been the scourge. Their descendants would later be numbered among the most pious of the Crusaders.

In Ireland there were still Vikings—a great confusion of Vikings. The original invaders who had conquered the principal cities had never become settlers in the same sense as the Northmen in England's Danelaw or in France's Normandy. The cities were trading centers and raiding bases, but the Vikings never conquered the country as a whole. During the tenth century, many Vikings who did not care to settle down in England or France came to Ireland in a new wave of invasion.

This led to years of fighting in Ireland between the new Vikings and the old Vikings. The Irish kings fought with both and with one another. To complete the confusion there was a fourth group, the so-called Foreign Irish. They were the product of intermarriage between the Irish and the Vikings, and their swords were for sale to the highest bidder. These men would fight on anybody's side, and they changed sides with great frequency.

This was the situation when Brian Boru came on the scene. Brian was the son of a minor Irish leader who

The knights in this twelfth-century Danish fresco are mounted on spirited steeds and carry pointed shields. They are among the last of the Vikings.

ruled a small province in what is now County Clare. Throughout his youth Brian fought the Danes at their headquarters in Limerick, hiding in caves and woods to waylay Vikings who ventured outside of the city's defenses. At one time his following was reduced to only fifteen men.

But, by the time he was in his mid-twenties, Brian's determination to conquer the foreigners had attracted volunteers from nearby provinces. He defeated the Viking King Ivar of Limerick in a pitched battle and freed that city from a foreign ruler. Ivar fled overseas but came back the next year and allied himself with the remaining Danes in southern Ireland and with certain disgruntled Irish chieftains. This time Ivar did not leave the battlefield alive; when the neighboring province of Leinster also submitted to Brian, he was overlord of all southern Ireland.

During the peaceful decade that followed his victories, Brian consolidated and reorganized his realm. Then, in the year 999, increasing hostilities in the north forced him to march on Dublin, where he conquered the Viking stronghold. Brian was lenient to the defeated Northmen. He accepted the submission of the local king, Sigtryg of the Silken Beard, who promised to support him if the Danes could have their own section of Dublin. When Brian continued his march north with his own men and the Danes of Dublin, the king of northern Ireland submitted without a fight, and Brian Boru became the high king of all Ireland, described in a chronicle of 1004 as Emperor of the Irish.

The next eight years were the most peaceful that Ireland had seen for over two centuries. The Northmen remained in the land, but nowhere did they rule. Then in 1012 revolt broke out in the province of Leinster, the king of which turned to Sigtryg for support.

Brian had made a mistake in pardoning the Viking king of Dublin. This turncoat hastened abroad to seek Viking aid. He promised Sigurd, chief of the Orkney Islands, the throne of Dublin in return for his help; he then made the same promise to Brodir, Viking chief of the Isle of Man. It was clear that this was to be a fight to the finish for Viking supremacy in Ireland, and Northmen gathered at Dublin from England and France, Wales and Scotland, Iceland and the Scandinavian countries.

Brian rallied the army from the rest of Ireland, and he too had some minor Viking support in ten ships from the Isle of Man. He gathered his host at Clontarf on a narrow neck of land between two rivers near Dublin. It was the mightiest army Ireland had ever seen, probably numbering

Brian Boru was able to defeat the Vikings in Ireland. As the Northmen withdrew, monks came out of their stone "beehive" cells (right, above); watchmen no longer looked out for foreign armies from their towers (above); and Ireland found peace. But rebellion then broke out in the province of Leinster—which is seen as the sharp, southeast corner in the medieval map of Ireland at right. To overcome the men of Leinster and their Viking allies, Brian marched on Dublin.

IRISH TOURIST OFFICE

BY PERMISSION OF THE TRUSTEES OF THE BRITISH MUSEUM

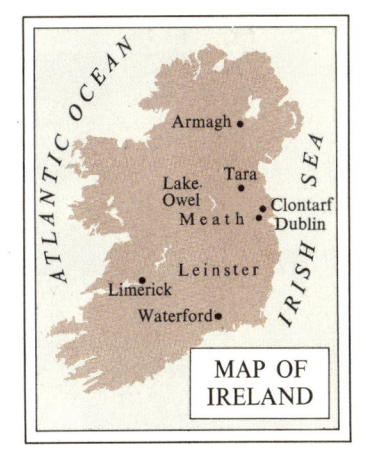

MAP OF IRELAND

The Viking on the black horse below is said to be Sigtryg, leader of the Northmen who were allied with the Leinster rebels against High King Brian. Brian, riding a white charger, attacks him. History gives the Battle of Clontarf somewhat differently—Brian took no part in the actual fighting—but he and Sigtryg were both dead by the end of the crucial battle.

about 20,000 men. The Leinster men with their Dublin and foreign Viking allies were approximately equal in number. But, as usual, the Vikings had the advantage in armor. The annals of Ireland say, "The foreigners of the west of Europe assembled against Brian; and they took with them ten hundred men with coats of mail. A spirited, fierce, violent, vengeful, and furious battle was fought between them—the likeness of which was not to be found at that time—on the Friday before Easter precisely."

Various old accounts of the battle differ, depending on who is telling the tale. All seem to agree that the Vikings made a tactical mistake by spreading their line too thin to cover their ships anchored in Dublin Bay—always a vital concern of Vikings—and the bridge over the Liffey River to Dublin. Most of the foreign Vikings were on the left flank, guarding the ships under Sigurd and Brodir, the two chieftains from the isles. The Dublin Vikings were on the

HAVERTY, *History of Ireland*, 1871

right, guarding the bridge under Sigtryg's brother. The Leinster rebels were in the center under their king. Brian's army was commanded by various kings from different parts of the country, with one section under his son and another under his fifteen-year-old grandson, Tordelbach. Because it was Good Friday, and perhaps because he was now seventy-three years old, Brian took no part in the fight. He retired to a nearby woods to spend the day in prayer.

The Leinster men were well placed on a hill and started the battle by sweeping down on the Irish center, driving it before them. This left the two Irish flanks completely isolated. The Dublin Vikings were quickly routed and the foreign Vikings pushed back until the ends of the Irish line could fold around the advancing Leinster men. These retreated in confusion from this exposed position. Sigurd and Brodir rallied their men, left their ships exposed, and went to the aid of the center. Their rush carried them through the Irish line and into the woods where Brian was praying. Brodir easily broke through the shield wall with which Brian's few followers tried to protect him and hacked down the old king, crying, "Now let man tell that Brodir felled Brian."

He had little time to rejoice. His band was now surrounded, and both he and Sigurd fell, as did Brian's son. The foreign Vikings tried to reach their ships, but few succeeded. The Irish pursued the fleeing Northmen into the water, and the annals say of Tordelbach, "The king's grandchild, but then of the age of fifteen years, was found drowned near the fishing weir of Clontarf with both hands fast bound in the hair of a Dane's head, whom he pursued to the sea at the time of the flight of the Danes."

Although it cost Ireland her first great king, together with his son and grandson, the Battle of Clontarf broke Viking hopes of conquering Ireland. Some of the Northmen stayed in Ireland, and there were a few later raids of the early pirate type. When the English conquered the land in the twelfth century, they mistreated Danes and Irish alike, and the last of the Vikings were absorbed in the common misery.

The Viking Era lasted longest in England. There, in the year 1000, the weak King Ethelred the Unready held the throne but hardly ruled. In the last twenty years of the tenth century the country was wracked by repeated large-scale raids. The first were led by Olaf Tryggvesson, who had been brought up in Novogorod and whose ninety-three ships were probably manned by Swedish Vikings from

England was still being raided by Northmen in the eleventh century. This raider from the end of the Viking Era is pictured as having high sides and an enclosed cabin.

Olaf Tryggvesson had a typically wide-ranging Viking career. Raised in Russia, he raided England, where he was baptized by Ethelred, then sailed on to Norway, which he unified by conquest. His successor, Olaf II, shown above receiving tribute from his people, was made a saint after his death.

Russia. Ethelred bought him off with Danegeld, baptized him, and Olaf returned to become the zealous Christian king of Norway.

Next came Sweyn Forkbeard, who was already king of Denmark. Year after year he attacked in a different section of England. Each time he was bribed to go home with larger Danegeld, only to return the following year.

In the year 1002 Ethelred once more paid Danegeld to rid himself of the Vikings. But, on hearing of a plot against his life, he unwisely broke the truce and ordered the slaughter of all Danes in England. The bloody massacre was carried out on St. Brice's Day of that same year, and among the victims was Gunhild, Sweyn's sister.

The enraged Danish king intensified his raids to avenge the death of his sister. The greatest attack took place in 1012 when Sweyn sent the Jomsvikings into England under their chief Thorkel the Tall and young Olaf Haroldson of Norway. This time Ethelred bought the Vikings off with the tremendous Danegeld of 48,000 pounds of silver. He also hired Thorkel, Olaf, and some of the Jomsvikings to remain in his service.

The loss of his lieutenants—and of the forty-five of his ships that they kept—persuaded Sweyn to change his tactics. He attacked England with a great army, rallied the Danes in the Danelaw, and swept through the land, subduing section after section whose lords usually submitted to his overpowering force without a struggle. This was a new type of Viking invasion—whereas Ivar and the chiefs of the Great Army had been content to let the English rule while they plundered, Sweyn was bent on national conquest. Before he died in 1014 he had overrun all of England, and Ethelred had fled to Normandy.

After the Danish king's death, the English recalled the unready Ethelred from his refuge with the Duke of Normandy and hailed him as king. Sweyn's twenty-year-old son Canute returned to Denmark for a larger army and came back the next year. Canute faced Ethelred's determined son Edmund Ironside, but the fierce young English patriot was defeated and forced to flee to stubbornly defended London. Here Ethelred, who had been too ill to fight, died, and Edmund was chosen king. After several more defeats, Edmund finally came to terms with Canute. The kingdom was divided into two uneasy parts, Canute receiving the larger share, including London. When Edmund died in 1016, the nobles turned to the remaining strong man and crowned Canute undisputed king of all England.

England's King Ethelred (above), called the Unready, had none of the boldness of his father, Edgar; he was content to buy off the Vikings with Danegeld. The penny at left below is dated 1008; the coin at right is also from Ethelred's reign.

BY PERMISSION OF THE TRUSTEES OF THE BRITISH MUSEUM

This was the peak of triumph of the Viking Era. Rollo had gained a province in France. Other Viking chiefs had ruled as kings in cities of Ireland and in sections of England. But Canute ruled an entire country—and for twenty years he ruled it well. To consolidate the kingdom and ally himself with the powerful Normans across the Channel, he married Ethelred's widow, Emma, sister of Duke William of Normandy. He declared he did not want England to be regarded as a colony, and to show his confidence in his new subjects he sent the Danish army home, keeping only a bodyguard of housecarls in England.

Canute's reign lasted until 1035. He was already king of Denmark, and he added the throne of Norway to his dominions. Scotland submitted to him and also the northern islands. This Viking king was an astute statesman as well as an able and just ruler. His reign was peaceful and constructive. Although he had been brought up among the Vikings, he permitted no Viking raids while he was king—and, with one important exception, there were no more Viking raids after he died.

The exception was in the year 1066. England was then ruled by Harold Godwinson, whose mother was half Danish and whose father had dominated Canute's successor, Edward the Confessor. Harold was a mighty figure, but he was plagued by his disloyal brother, Tostig, who felt he had an equal right to be king. Seeking support for his claim, Tostig journeyed among his mother's people in the Northland.

He found a ready ear in Harold Hardrada, who was not loath to take the crown of England away from its rightful owner—to put it on his own head, not Tostig's. Tostig was willing to take second place, and he told Harold that he could induce several of the English earls to declare for him if he landed with a sufficiently strong army. Harold called out half of the Viking host and sailed for England with two hundred ships, picking up reinforcements from the Scottish isles on the way.

After winning a few skirmishes along the coast, Harold sailed up the Humber to attack York. First he won an easy battle outside the city, then Tostig induced the garrison to surrender. It was arranged for the Vikings to take possession of the castle the next day. They returned to their ships and celebrated. The next day dawned clear and hot; so hot in

Serpents' heads, such as the one above, were placed in the bows of Viking fighting ships before battles to ward off evil spirits.

King Canute, crowned by an angel, honors his new land by placing a golden English-style cross on the altar of a church. His queen is at far left.

BY PERMISSION OF THE TRUSTEES OF THE BRITISH MUSEUM

fact that two thirds of the men that Harold took toward York with him did not wear their armor. They expected to do some drinking and perhaps some plundering but no fighting.

The Vikings did not know that the situation in York had changed during the night. Harold of England had arrived with his host and entered the city. As the Vikings marched casually toward their goal, a cloud of dust advanced from the city to meet them. Through it they could see the glint of sun on armor. Tostig advised retiring to the ships; Harold, who had never been defeated by Slavs or Saracens, Greeks or Sicilians, would have no part of this cautious advice. The two kings deployed their forces at Stamford Bridge—the half-Danish Harold of England faced the Norwegian Viking. Before the battle, twenty armored knights rode forward from the English line, and the leader called to Tostig, saying that his brother offered him the earldom of Northumbria if he would make peace.

"And what," said Tostig, "does my brother offer my ally, Harold of Norway?"

"To Harold of Norway, Harold of England will give seven feet of English ground, or as much more as he may be taller than other men," was the reply.

When battle was joined, it was a hard and bloody one. The English charged the Viking shield wall and were repulsed, but when the Vikings broke the wall to pursue, their unarmored bodies were soft targets for English arrows. As they fell around him, the giant Harold seemed

At the Battle of Stamford Bridge, the English king Harold defeated the Viking Harold Hardrada. A generation earlier, the Viking king Canute (below, at right) had routed England's Edmund Ironside (left).

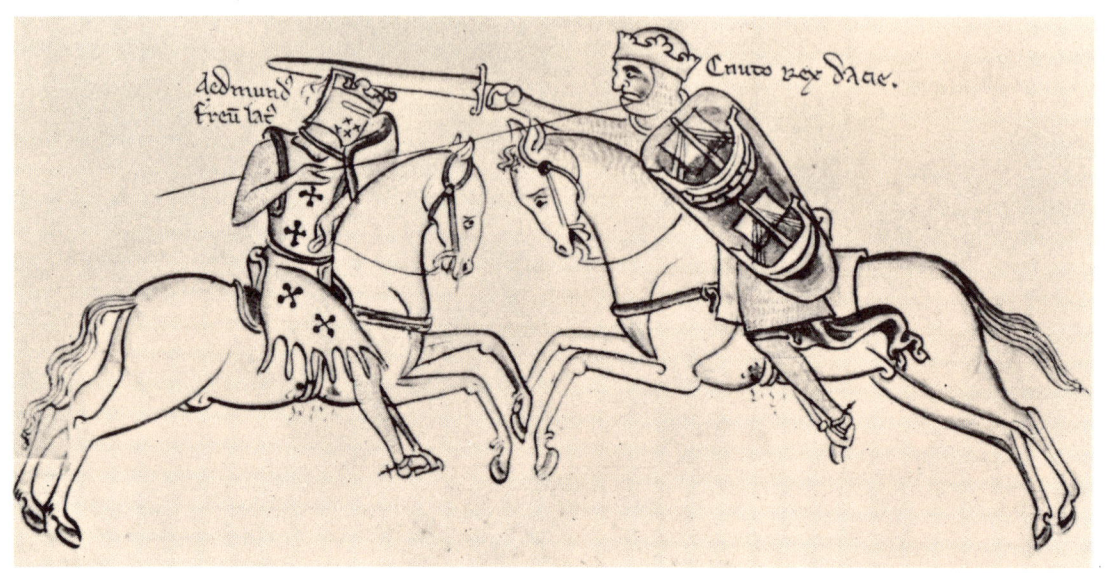

BY PERMISSION OF THE MASTER, LIBRARIAN, AND FELLOWS OF CORPUS CHRISTI COLLEGE, CAMBRIDGE

144

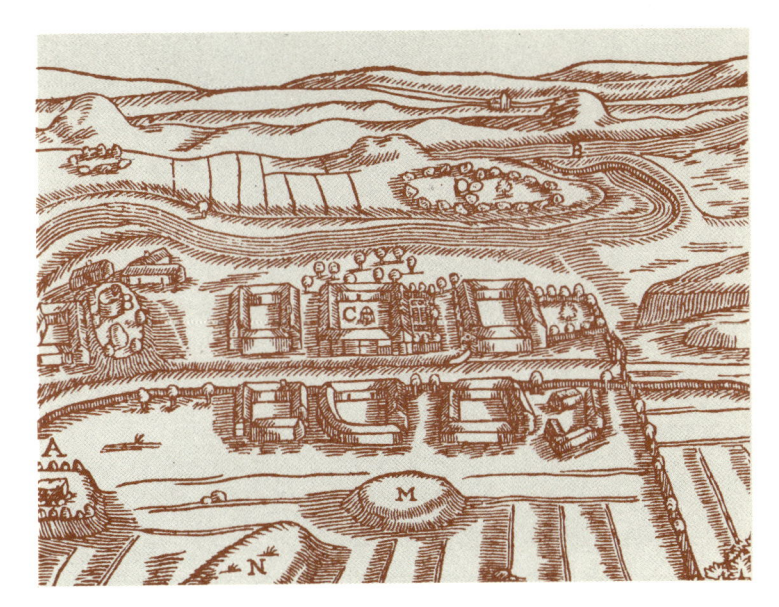

At right is a seventeenth-century reconstruction of the remains of a Viking community in Denmark. The letter "C" marks a hall for huge banquets, four typical Viking houses joined together. At "M" is a mound where the gods Odin and Thor were still worshiped.

to go berserk and charged forward, cutting a swath through the enemy with great sweeps of his broadsword. His men rallied behind him, and the English started to fall back in confusion. Then an arrow found its mark in Harold's unprotected throat, and he fell to win his seven feet of English ground, the last true Viking chieftain to die on foreign soil.

Harold of England's triumph was short-lived. An even more dangerous enemy was approaching to the south—Duke William of Normandy, great-great-grandson of the Viking Rollo. Harold hastened to face him with his depleted, battle-weary army, and a few days later, fell at the Battle of Hastings.

This famous battle of the Norman Conquest was no Viking affair, but, in a sense, it was an outcome of the Viking movement. Had there been no Vikings, there would have been neither a William the Conqueror nor a Harold of England, for Viking blood flowed strongly in the veins of both; and many of the men who fought with them on both sides could trace descent from the followers of Rollo in France and Ivar the Boneless in England and to the many Vikings who had later swelled the settlements in both countries. Even the Norman standard bearer bore, along with William's banner, a Scandinavian name, Thurstan, son of Rolf.

In the sagas there is an interesting sequel to the Battle of Hastings. It is told that before Ivar the Boneless died in

TEXT CONTINUED ON PAGE 148

REGIS: HIC CECIDERUNT

In the Norman Conquest of England, the Viking-descended warriors of Duke William of Normandy used an old tactic in which defenders were provoked to break ranks and pursue, and were then cut off. This section of the famous Bayeux Tapestry shows English footsoldiers with battle-axes (standing at left) isolated on a hillock and surrounded by sword-swinging Norman knights.

TEXT CONTINUED FROM PAGE 145

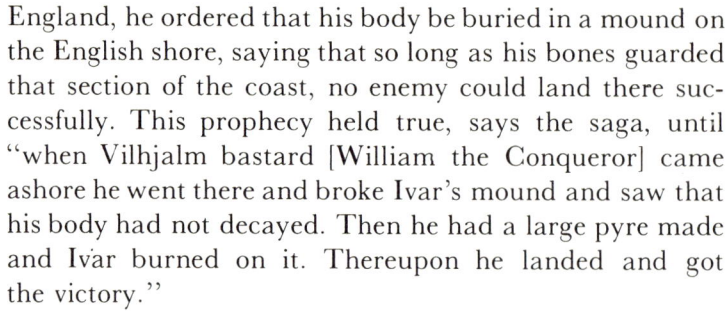

England, he ordered that his body be buried in a mound on the English shore, saying that so long as his bones guarded that section of the coast, no enemy could land there successfully. This prophecy held true, says the saga, until "when Vilhjalm bastard [William the Conqueror] came ashore he went there and broke Ivar's mound and saw that his body had not decayed. Then he had a large pyre made and Ivar burned on it. Thereupon he landed and got the victory."

History pays little heed to the few puny Viking pirate raids after the Norman Conquest. They were relics of an era that had ended. The countries of Western Europe were no longer disorganized, easy prey to plundering Northmen, and the Northmen were no longer pagan strangers. There were no longer undefended coastlines that invited rovers to go *i viking*. The Northmen had become Christian neighbors of their original victims.

Those who had come to raid, and then stayed on to settle, left little in the way of material monuments—a few skeletons and hundreds of Scandinavian place names in England and Normandy. Yet they did make intangible but positive contributions to the progress of European civilization. First, the Vikings played a part in the naval tradition that aided in the development of Western Europe after the Viking Era. The mighty fleets of France were largely staffed by seamen from Normandy and its neighboring province of Brittany, and England's rule of the waves for so many centuries owes much to the Vikings and Normans who successively conquered her. Also, the Northmen left a lasting imprint upon English law, upon which American law in turn is based.

But perhaps their most important contribution stems from the Vikings' strong feeling of personal equality and individual freedom. When Rollo landed in France, his men were asked the name of their lord. They replied, "We have no lord, we are all equal." And after the feudal period, Normandy was the first French province to give up serfdom. Freedom and equality ultimately became the most important heritage of both France and England, and of the colonies they formed in America. The Vikings, who helped destroy the civilization that Europe had inherited from Rome, also helped found a new world.

The stone carving at right honors Magnus the Great, one of the last Viking kings of Norway. The cross above, symbolic of the new Christian spirit that swept the Northland, was unearthed in the Greenland Viking colony.

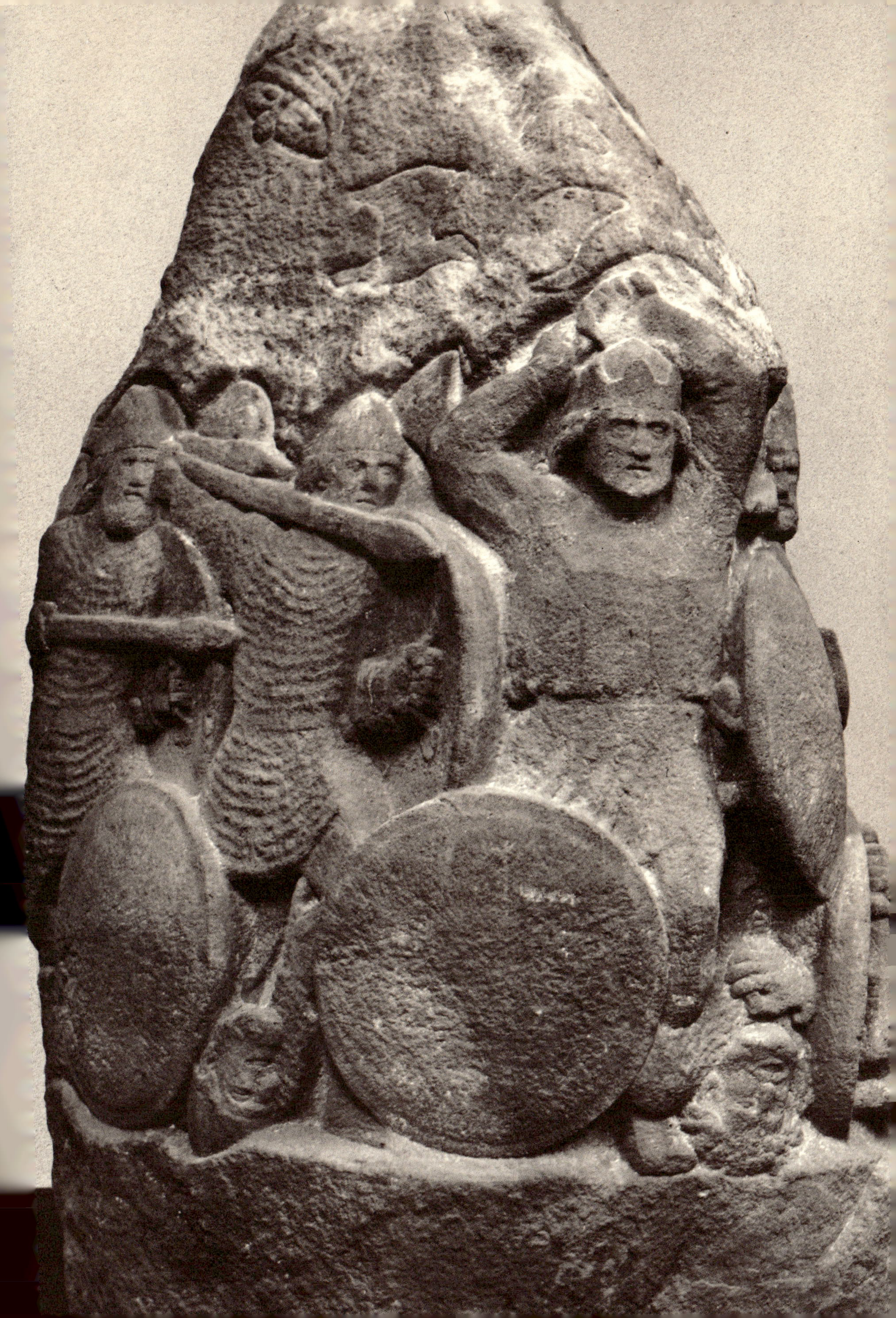

ACKNOWLEDGMENTS

The Editors are deeply grateful to the curators of the American and European collections in which rare examples of Viking and medieval art are to be found. Foremost among these are the national collections of the Scandinavian countries, from which the Vikings came, and those of Ireland, England, Iceland, and France, where the Vikings settled. Special thanks are owed to the following individuals and organizations for their assistance and for making available material in their collections:

Mrs. Erna Aasheim, Universitetets Oldsaksamling, Oslo

S. Rinman, Kungl. Vitterhets Historie och Antikvitets Akademien, Stockholm

Mrs. Maj Odelberg, Riksantikvarieambetet och Statens Historiska Museum, Stockholm

Fritze Lindahl, National Museum, Copenhagen

Eric J. Friis, American Scandinavian Society

Dr. Kristján Eldjárn, National Museum of Iceland

National Museum of Antiquities of Scotland

Mrs. Mary Frances Rhymer, Chicago Historical Society

Michael Boretsky

Dr. Frederick Dockstader, Museum of the American Indian, Heye Foundation

William Forsyth, Metropolitan Museum of Art

René Cuenot, Bibliothèque Municipale de Nancy

Dr. Christophe von Steiger, Burgerbibliothek, Bern

A. T. Lucas, National Museum of Ireland

Departments of British and Medieval Antiquities, Coins and Medals, Map Room of the British Museum

Charles M. Boland

Vatican Library

Fabrizio Parisio, Naples

Padre T. Leccisotti, Abbey of Monte Cassino, Italy

A. B. Allhems Forlag, Malmo, Sweden

George McGrath, Wesley Associates

Hannes Kjartansson, Consul General of Iceland

Dr. John L. Mish and Roman Ilnytzky, New York Public Library, Slavonic Division

Special research and photography: England—Susanne Puddefoot, Maureen Green; Italy—Maria Todorow; New York—Geoffrey Clements

Maps by Herbert Borst

AMERICAN HERITAGE PUBLISHING CO., INC.

James Parton, *President*

Joseph J. Thorndike, Jr., *Editorial Director*

Richard M. Ketchum, *Editor, Book Division*

Irwin Glusker, *Art Director*

HORIZON CARAVEL BOOKS

RUSSELL BOURNE, *Managing Editor*

Janet Czarnetzki, *Art Director*

Mervyn Kaufman, *Associate Editor*

Judith Harkison, *Chief Picture Researcher*

Lucy Davidson Rosenfeld, *Picture Researcher*

Elaine K. Andrews, *Copy Editor*

Nancy Simon, *Editorial Assistant*

Gertrudis Feliu, *Chief, European Bureau*

FURTHER REFERENCE

Although there are few Viking relics in American collections, Viking ship models can be seen in the following museums: The Smithsonian Institution, Washington, D.C., the Peabody Museum, Salem, Mass., and the Mystic Seaport Marine Historical Association, Mystic, Conn. Viking weapons and implements are included in the collections of The Metropolitan Museum of Art, New York City, the United States Naval Academy, Annapolis, Md., and the Royal Ontario Museum of the University of Toronto. The Runestone Museum in Alexandria, Minn., contains the controversial Kensington Stone as well as numerous tools and weapons of possible Viking origin. Early medieval art of the period can be found in the collections of the Walters Art Gallery, Baltimore, Md., the Pierpont Morgan Library, New York City, the Free Library of Philadelphia, and the Cloisters Collection of The Metropolitan Museum of Art.

For those who wish to read further on the Vikings and the Viking Era, the following books are recommended:

Arbman, Holger. *The Vikings*. Frederick A. Praeger, 1961.
Boland, Charles Michael. *They All Discovered America*. Permabook Edition, 1963.
Brondsted, Johannes. *The Vikings*. Penguin Books, 1960.
Duckett, Eleanor Shipley. *Alfred the Great*. Univ. of Chicago Press, 1956.
Guignebert, Charles. *A Short History of the French People*. George Allen and Unwin, Ltd., 1930.
Jones, Gwyn. *The North Atlantic Saga*. Oxford University Press, 1964.
Kendrick, T. D. *A History of the Vikings*. Scribner's Sons, 1930.
Kendrick, T. D. *Late Saxon and Viking Art*. Methuen & Co., Ltd., 1949.
Loyn, H. R. *Anglo-Saxon England and the Norman Conquest*. St. Martin's Press, 1962.
Pares, Bernard. *A History of Russia*. Alfred A. Knopf, 1960.
Pohl, Frederick J. *Atlantic Crossings Before Columbus*. W. W. Norton & Co., 1961.
Sawyer, P. H. *The Age of the Vikings*. St. Martin's Press, 1962.
Vernadsky, George. *Ancient Russia*. Yale University Press, 1959.
Winston, Richard. *Charlemagne—From the Hammer to the Cross*. Vintage Books, 1954.

This ancient Swedish rune stone, with its simple ship and horseman, dates from the late eighth century.

INDEX

Bold face indicates pages on which maps or illustrations appear

A

Adam of Bremen, 129
   manuscript of, **119**
Aix-la-Chapelle, 11
Alfred Jewel, **45**
Alfred the Great, 43, 45–46, **46**, 47, 51–53, 96, 101
Althing, 101, 102, 107
America, discovery of, 7, 15, 113–132
Ancient Chronicle, 64, 68, 71
Anglo-Saxon Chronicle, 24
Armagh, Ireland, 29
Arnarson, Ingolf, **98**, 98, 99
Arnarson, Leif, 98–99
Art, Viking, 7, **22**, **37**, **80**, **95**
Asa, Queen, 89
Ashdown, Wessex, 45
Askold (Viking chief), **64**, 68, 69

B

Baffin Island, 131
Baltic Sea, 63, 64
Barents, Willem, 98
Barents Sea, 98
Bass River, **128**
Battle-axes, **24**, 24, 78, **84**, 85
Beaduheard, 26
Berserkers, 37–38
Bertric, King, 26
Biorn, Emil, painting by, **113**
Bjarni Herjulfson, 116–117; **118**, 122, 128
Bjorn Ironside, 40–41
Black Sea, 68, 80
Bordeaux, France, 40
Brendan (monk), 98
Brian Boru, 135–139, **138**
Brodir (Viking chief), 136, 138, 139
Buildings, Viking, 88
Burial customs, 85–86, 89

C

Caesar, 11, 19
Calder, A. S., statue of Leif Ericson by, **119**
Canute, King, 7, 88, 141, 142, **143**, **144**
Charlemagne, **10**, **11**, 11–12, **13**, 32–33, 43, 55, 101
Charles the Bald, 33, 37, **42**, 43, 55

Charles the Fat, 55, 56, 60
Charles the Simple, 60
Christianity, 33, 98, 104, 106–107, 111
Clontarf, Battle of, 136, 138–139
Constantinople, **67**, 68, 71, 72, 74, 77
Costumes, Viking, **38**, **39**, 80, 84, 87

D

Danegeld, 46, 141
Danelaw, 47, 51, 53, 68, 135, 141
Dark Ages, 7
Denmark, 7, **14**, 19, 22, 24, 53, 142
Dighton Rock, **129**
Dir (Viking chief), **64**, 68, 69
Drevlianians, 72
Dublin, Ireland, 136, 137

E

East Anglia, 41–45, 53
Edgar, King, **46**
Edmund, King, 7, **44**, 44–45, 141, **144**
Edward, King, 53
Edward the Confessor, 142
Emma, Queen, 142, **143**
England, 7, **14**, 23, 26, 28, 32, 43–49, **50, 51**, 51–53, 63, 68, 77, 88, 100, 135, 139, 141, 142, 144–145, 148
Eric IX, King, **6**, 7
Eric the Red, 107, 111, 122
   ship of, **111**
Ericson, Leif, **110**, 110–111, 113–**118**, **118**, **119**, **121**, 127, 128, 131–132, 135
   ship of, **cover**
Ericson, Thorstein, 122
Ericson, Thorvald, 118, 122
Ethelred, King, 45
Ethelred the Unready, 23, 139, **141**, 141
Explorers, Viking, 7, 15, 97–111

F

Fadlar, Ibn, 86
Flatey Book, **103**, 116, 128
Floki, 98
Forannan, Bishop, 29
France, 33–36, 40, 43, 55–60, 135,

142, 148
Frey (god), 19
Freydis (daughter of Eric the Red), 122, 126, 127–128, 131
Frigg (goddess), 19

G

Garonne River, 40
Gizur the White, 107
Godfred of Denmark, 32–33
Gods, Viking, 19, **19**
Gotland, 78
Gnupsson, Eric, 132
Great Army, 43–44, 63, 141
Greeks, 71–72
Greenland, 7, 15, 107, **108**, 110, 111, 116, 122, 127, 128, 131, 132
Gunhild, 141
Guthrum (Viking chief), 46, 47, **101**

H

Halfdan (Viking chief), 46
Hardrada, Harold, 72, 74, 77, 142, 144–145
Harold Bluetooth, 55
Harold Fairhair, 99–100, 101
Harold of Denmark, 33
Harold of England, 142, 144–145
Hastings (Viking chief), 41, 51
Hastings, Battle of, 145
Hauk's Book, 116, 128
Helmets, Viking, **23, 82, 84, 85**, 85
Herjulf, 116–117

I

Iceland, 7, 15, 98–107, **99**, 100, 116, 132
Igor, **68**, 71, 72
Indians, American, 118, 123–124, **125**, 126, 130
Ingstad, Dr. Helge, 113, **115**, 115, 128, 131
Ireland, **28**, 28–32, 36, 38, 43, 98, 100, 123, 127, 135–139, **137**, 142
Isle of Man, 26, 136
Italy, 41
Ivar of Limerick, 136
Ivar the Boneless, 7, 40, 44–45, 68, 141, 145, 148

152

J

Jerusalem, 74
Jocelin, Bishop of Paris, 55
Jomsvikings, 53, 141

K

Karlsefni, Thorfinn, **113,** 122–124, **123,** 126–127, 129, 130
Kensington Stone, 132, **133**
Khazars, 69
Kiev, 68, 69, 74, 77
Knights, **18,** 53, 60, **81, 92, 134**
Krohg, Christian, painting by, **120–121**

L

Labrador, 131
L'Anse aux Meadows, Newfoundland, 113, 115
Lea River, 51
Leo III, Pope, 11, **13**
Limerick, Ireland, 136
Lindisfarne (island), 26
Literature, Viking, 7, 22–24, 113, 116, 128
Logberg (Law Mount), **100,** 102
Loire River, 33, 36, 39
London, England, 23–24, 141
Lothair, 33
Louis the German, 33
Louis the Pious, **32,** 33, **33**
Luna, Italy, 41

M

Magnus the Good, 77
Magnus the Great, **149**
Michael III, Emperor, 68
Michael V, Emperor, 77
Moors, **40,** 41
Morocco, 41

N

Nantes, France, 33, 39
Nekor, Morocco, 41
Nestor (monk), **69**
Newfoundland, 113, 115, 131
Newport, Rhode Island, tower, **127,** 132
Noirmoutier (island), 36
Normandy, Duke of, 60
North America, map of, **130**
North Cape, 97–98
Northumbria, 44
Norway, 7, 32, 74, 77, 89, 98, 99, 101, 110, 111, 142
Nova Scotia, 131

Novgorod, 63, 64

O

Odin (god), **19,** 19, 37
Olaf II of Norway (*also called* Olaf Haroldson and Saint Olaf), 23, 24, 74, **140,** 141
Olaf the White (Viking chief in Ireland), 32
Olaf Tryggvesson, 94, 106–107, 111, 122, 139, 140, 141
Oleg (Viking chief), 69, 71
Olga, **68,** 72
Orkney Islands, 15, 131, 136, 142
Ota, 30
Ottar of Norway, 97
Owel, Lake, 31

P

Paris, France, 55–56, **57,** 60
Patzinaks, 69
Pisa, Italy, 41

R

Ragnar Lodbrok, 38–39
Rhone River, 41
Richard, 60
Rollo, **59,** 60, **60,** 142, 145, 148
Roman Empire, 11–12, 19, 32–33
Rome, Italy, 41
Rune stones, **41,** 86–89, 132, **151**
Rurik, 64, **68,** 68, 69
Russia, 7, 38, 63–64, **65,** 68–72, 78, 80, 98, 135

S

Sagas, 22–23, 24, 37, 38, 53, 78, 80, 82, 85, 88, 94, 102, 105, 113, 116–117, 128, 130–131, 145
Scandinavia, **13,** 19, 22, 24, 53, 64
Schiott, painting by, **102**
Scotland, **14,** 26, 32, **50,** 142
Seine Vikings, 36
Severn River, 53
Shetland Islands, 15, 131, 142
Shields, Viking, **26, 27, 29,** 80, 81, 84, 85, 93
Ships, Viking, **cover,** 7, **8–9,** 12, 15, **16–17,** 19, 22, 23, 29, 33, 37, 41, **41, 48–49,** 51, **54,** 55, **58, 61, 62–63,** 63, **64,** 71, **73, 78, 79, 89, 90,** 90, 91, **93,** 93–94, **95, 96,** 139, **139**
Sicily, 74
Siegfried (Viking chief), 55, 56
Sigurd (Viking chief), 136, 138, 139
Skylitzes, John, manuscript by, **70**
Slavs, 63, 64, 68, 69, 72
Spain, 41

Stamford Bridge, Battle of, 144
Straumfjord, 122, 126
Svyatoslav, 72, **75**
Swanage Bay, Battle of, **48–49**
Sweden, 77
Sweyn, King, 129
Sweyn, Forkbeard, 141
Swords, Viking, **27, 36, 38,** 80, 82, 85

T

Tapestries, **endsheets, 20–21,** 86, 87, 106, 146–147
Tara, Ireland, **30**
Thames River, 23, 24, 51, 78
Thetford, England, **29**
Thingvellir (Plain of the Parliament), **100,** 102
Thor (god), 19, **107,** 123
  hammer symbol of, **title page,** 19
Thorgilsson, Ari, 129
Thorhall the Hunter, 122–123
Thorkel the Tall, 141
Thorvard, 122, 127, 128, 130–131
Thurstan, 145
Tordelbach, 139
Tostig, 142, 144
Toulouse, France, 40
Tours, France, 40
Turgeis (Viking chief), 29–32, 39
Tyrkir, 118, **118**

V

Valkyries, 37, **92**
Varangian Guard, 74, 77, 89
Viking Era, 7, 15, 19, 22, 23, 36, 55, 78, 135, 139, 142
Vinland, *see* Wineland
Vittefarne, Ingvar, 88

W

Wessex, England, 45–47, 53
William, Duke of Normandy, 145, 148
William Longsword, 60
Wineland (Vinland), 118, 119, 127, 129, 131–132
Woden, *see* Odin

Y

Yaroslav, 64
York, England, 44, 142, 144

Z

Zealand, 53
Zoë, Empress, 77

153

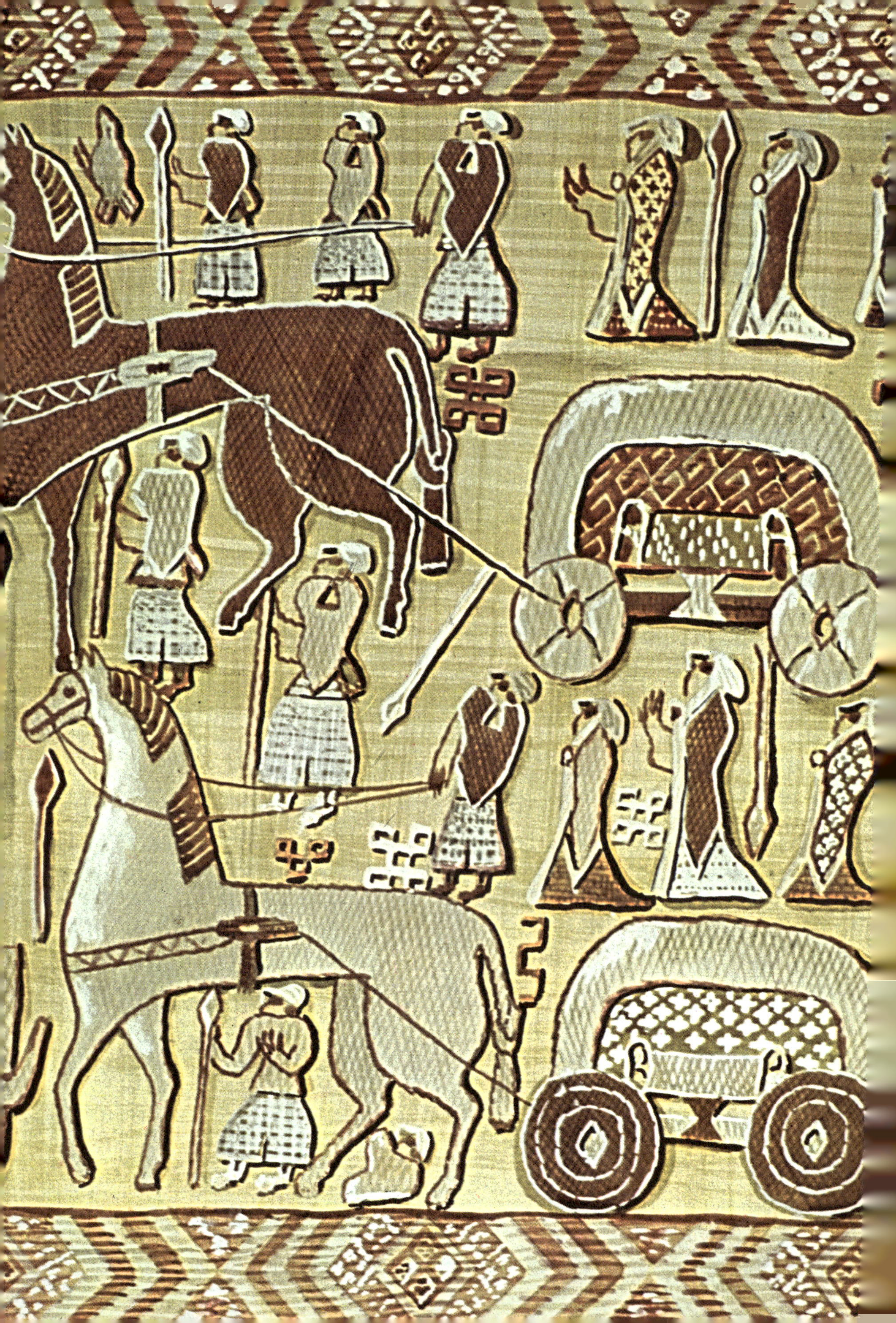